An Unction from the Holy One

An Unction from the Holy One

4ink7

ISBN: 978-1-943661-03-9

An Unction from the Holy One is Issue One of 4ink7, a literary journal that is a book. Individually, all rights revert to the authors upon publication.

Printed in the USA

4ink7
PO BOX 4945
Chattanooga, TN 37405

Contents

Ambrose Bierce

AN OCCURRENCE AT OWL CREEK BRIDGE

A man stood upon a railroad bridge in northern Alabama, looking down into the swift water twenty feet below. The man's hands were behind his back, the wrists bound with a cord. A rope closely encircled his neck. It was attached to a stout cross-timber above his head and the slack fell to the level of his knees. Some loose boards laid upon the ties supporting the rails of the railway supplied a footing for him and his executioners—two private soldiers of the Federal army, directed by a sergeant who in civil life may have been a deputy sheriff. At a short remove upon the same temporary platform was an officer in the uniform of his rank, armed. He was a captain. A sentinel at each end of the bridge stood with his rifle in the position known as "support," that is to say, vertical in front of the left shoulder, the hammer resting on the forearm thrown straight across the chest—a formal and unnatural position, enforcing an erect carriage of the body. It did not appear to be the duty of these two men to know what was occurring at the center of the bridge; they merely blockaded the two ends of the foot planking that traversed it.

Beyond one of the sentinels nobody was in sight; the railroad ran straight away into a forest for a hundred yards, then, curving, was lost to view. Doubtless there was an outpost farther along. The other bank of the stream was open ground—a gentle slope topped with a stockade of vertical tree trunks, loopholed for rifles, with a single embrasure through which protruded the muzzle of a brass cannon commanding the bridge. Midway up the slope between the bridge and fort were the spectators—a single company of infantry in line, at "parade rest," the butts of their rifles on the ground, the barrels inclining slightly backward against the right shoulder, the hands crossed upon the stock. A lieutenant stood at the right of the line, the point of his sword upon the ground, his left hand resting upon his right. Excepting the group of four at the center of the bridge, not a man moved. The company faced the bridge, staring stonily, motionless. The sentinels, facing the banks of the stream, might have been statues to adorn the bridge. The captain stood with folded arms, silent, observing the work of his subordinates, but making no sign. Death is a dignitary who when he comes announced is to be received with formal manifestations of respect, even by those most familiar with him. In the code of military etiquette silence and fixity are forms of deference.

The man who was engaged in being hanged was apparently about thirty-five years of age. He was a civilian, if one might judge from his habit, which was that of a planter. His features were good—a straight nose, firm mouth, broad forehead, from which his long, dark hair was combed straight back, falling behind his ears to the collar of his well fitting frock coat. He wore a mustache and pointed beard, but no whiskers; his eyes were large and dark gray, and had a kindly expression which one would hardly have expected in one whose neck was in the hemp. Evidently this was no vulgar assassin. The liberal military code makes provision for hanging many kinds of persons, and gentlemen are not excluded.

The preparations being complete, the two private soldiers stepped aside and each drew away the plank upon which he had been standing. The sergeant turned to the captain, saluted and placed himself immediately behind that officer, who in turn moved apart one pace. These movements left the condemned man and the sergeant standing on the two ends of the same plank, which spanned three of the cross-ties of the bridge. The end upon which the civilian stood almost, but not quite, reached a fourth. This plank had been held in place by the weight of the captain; it was now held by that of the sergeant. At a signal from the former the latter would step aside, the plank would tilt and the condemned man go down between two ties. The arrangement commended itself to his judgment as simple and effective. His face had not been covered nor his eyes bandaged. He looked a moment at his "unsteadfast footing," then let his gaze wander to the swirling water of the stream racing madly beneath his feet. A piece of dancing driftwood caught his attention and his eyes followed it down the current. How slowly it appeared to move! What a sluggish stream!

He closed his eyes in order to fix his last thoughts upon his wife and children. The water, touched to gold by the early sun, the brooding mists under the banks at some distance down the stream, the fort, the soldiers, the piece of drift—all had distracted him. And now he became conscious of a new disturbance. Striking through the thought of his dear ones was sound which he could neither ignore nor understand, a sharp, distinct, metallic percussion like the stroke of a blacksmith's hammer upon the anvil; it had the same ringing quality. He wondered what it was, and whether immeasurably distant or near by—it seemed both. Its recurrence was regular, but as slow as the tolling of a death knell. He awaited each new stroke with impatience and—he knew not why—apprehension. The intervals of silence grew progressively longer; the delays became maddening. With their greater infrequency the sounds increased in strength and sharpness. They hurt his ear like the trust of a knife; he feared he would shriek. What he heard was the ticking of his watch.

He unclosed his eyes and saw again the water below him. "If I could free my hands," he thought, "I might throw off the noose and spring into the stream. By diving I could evade the bullets and, swimming vigorously, reach the bank, take to the woods and get away home. My home, thank God, is as yet outside their lines; my wife and little ones are still beyond the invader's farthest advance."

As these thoughts, which have here to be set down in words, were flashed into the doomed man's brain rather than evolved from it the captain nodded to the sergeant. The sergeant stepped aside.

II

Peyton Farquhar was a well to do planter, of an old and highly respected Alabama family. Being a slave owner and like other slave owners a politician, he was naturally an original secessionist and ardently devoted to the Southern cause. Circumstances of an imperious nature, which it is unnecessary to relate here, had prevented him from taking service with that gallant army which had fought the disastrous campaigns ending with the fall of Corinth, and he chafed under the inglorious restraint, longing for the release of his energies, the larger life of the soldier, the opportunity for distinction. That opportunity, he felt, would come, as it comes to all in wartime. Meanwhile he did what he could. No service was too humble for him to perform in the aid of the South, no adventure too perilous for him to undertake if consistent with the character of a civilian who was at heart a soldier, and who in good faith and without too much qualification assented to at least a part of the frankly villainous dictum that all is fair in love and war.

One evening while Farquhar and his wife were sitting on a rustic bench near the entrance to his grounds, a gray-clad soldier rode up to the gate and asked for a drink of water. Mrs. Farquhar was only too happy to serve him with her own white hands. While she was fetching the water her husband approached the dusty horseman and inquired eagerly for news from the front.

"The Yanks are repairing the railroads," said the man, "and are getting ready for another advance. They have reached the Owl Creek bridge, put it in order and built a stockade on the north bank. The commandant has issued an order, which is posted everywhere, declaring that any civilian caught interfering with the railroad, its bridges, tunnels, or trains will be summarily hanged. I saw the order."

"How far is it to the Owl Creek bridge?" Farquhar asked.

"About thirty miles."

"Is there no force on this side of the creek?"

"Only a picket post half a mile out, on the railroad, and a single sentinel at this end of the bridge."

"Suppose a man—a civilian and student of hanging—should elude the picket post and perhaps get the better of the sentinel," said Farquhar, smiling, "what could he accomplish?"

The soldier reflected. "I was there a month ago," he replied. "I observed that the flood of last winter had lodged a great quantity of driftwood against the wooden pier at this end of the bridge. It is now dry and would burn like tinder."

The lady had now brought the water, which the soldier drank. He thanked her ceremoniously, bowed to her husband and rode away. An hour later, after nightfall, he re-passed the plantation, going northward in the direction from which he had come. He was a Federal scout.

III

As Peyton Farquhar fell straight downward through the bridge he lost consciousness and was as one already dead. From this state he was awakened—ages later, it seemed to him—by the pain of a sharp pressure upon his throat, followed by a sense of suffocation. Keen, poignant agonies seemed to shoot from his neck downward through every fiber of his body and limbs. These pains appeared to flash along well defined lines of ramification and to beat with an inconceivably rapid periodicity. They seemed like streams of pulsating fire heating him to an intolerable temperature. As to his head, he was conscious of nothing but a feeling of fullness—of congestion. These sensations were unaccompanied by thought. The intellectual part of his nature was already effaced; he had power only to feel, and feeling was torment. He was conscious of motion. Encompassed in a luminous cloud, of which he was now merely the fiery heart, without material substance, he swung through unthinkable arcs of oscillation, like a vast pendulum. Then all at once, with terrible suddenness, the light about him shot upward with the noise of a loud splash; a frightful roaring was in his ears, and all was cold and dark. The power of thought was restored; he knew that the rope had broken and he had fallen into the stream. There was no additional strangulation; the noose about his neck was already suffocating him and kept the water from his lungs. To die of hanging at the bottom of a river!—the idea seemed to him ludicrous. He opened his eyes in the darkness and saw above him a gleam of light, but how distant, how inaccessible! He was still sinking, for the light became fainter and fainter until it was a mere glimmer. Then it began to grow and brighten, and he knew that he was rising toward the surface—knew it with reluctance, for he was now very comfortable. "To be hanged and drowned," he thought, "that is not so bad; but I do not wish to be shot. No; I will not be shot; that is not fair."

He was not conscious of an effort, but a sharp pain in his wrist apprised him that he was trying to free his hands. He gave the struggle his attention, as an idler might observe the feat of a juggler, without interest in the outcome. What splendid effort!—what magnificent, what superhuman strength! Ah, that was a fine endeavor! Bravo! The cord fell away; his arms parted and floated upward, the hands dimly seen on each side in the growing light. He watched them with a new interest as first one and then the other pounced upon the noose at his neck. They tore it away and thrust it fiercely aside, its undulations resembling those of a water snake. "Put it back, put it back!" He thought he shouted these words to his hands, for the undoing of the noose had been succeeded by the direst pang that he had yet experienced. His neck ached horribly; his brain was on fire, his heart, which had been fluttering faintly, gave a great leap, trying to force itself out at his mouth. His whole body was racked and wrenched with an insupportable anguish! But his disobedient hands gave no heed to the command. They beat the water vigorously with quick, downward strokes, forcing him to the surface. He felt his head emerge; his eyes were blinded by the sunlight; his chest expanded convulsively, and with a supreme and crowning agony his lungs engulfed a great draught of air, which instantly he expelled in a shriek!

He was now in full possession of his physical senses. They were, indeed, preternaturally keen and alert. Something in the awful disturbance of his organic system had so exalted and refined them that they made record of things never before perceived. He felt the ripples upon his face and heard their separate sounds as they struck. He looked at the forest on the bank of the stream, saw the individual trees, the leaves and the veining of each leaf—he saw the very insects upon them: the locusts, the brilliant bodied flies, the gray spiders stretching their webs from twig to twig. He noted the prismatic colors in all the dewdrops upon a million blades of grass. The humming of the gnats that danced above the eddies of the stream, the beating of the dragon flies' wings, the strokes of the water spiders' legs, like oars which had lifted their boat—all these made audible music. A fish slid along beneath his eyes and he heard the rush of its body parting the water.

He had come to the surface facing down the stream; in a moment the visible world seemed to wheel slowly round, himself the pivotal point, and he saw the bridge, the fort, the soldiers upon the bridge, the captain, the sergeant, the two privates, his executioners. They were in silhouette against the blue sky. They shouted and gesticulated, pointing at him. The captain had drawn his pistol, but did not fire; the others were unarmed. Their movements were grotesque and horrible, their forms gigantic.

Suddenly he heard a sharp report and something struck the water smartly within a few inches of his head, spattering his face with spray. He heard a second report, and saw one of the sentinels with his rifle at his shoulder, a light cloud of blue smoke rising from the muzzle. The man in the water saw the eye of the man on the bridge gazing into his own through the sights of the rifle. He observed that it was a gray eye and remembered having read that gray eyes were keenest, and that all famous marksmen had them. Nevertheless, this one had missed.

A counter-swirl had caught Farquhar and turned him half round; he was again looking at the forest on the bank opposite the fort. The sound of a clear, high voice in a monotonous singsong now rang out behind him and came across the water with a distinctness that pierced and subdued all other sounds, even the beating of the ripples in his ears. Although no soldier, he had frequented camps enough to know the dread significance of that deliberate, drawling, aspirated chant; the lieutenant on shore was taking a part in the morning's work. How coldly and pitilessly—with what an even, calm intonation, presaging, and enforcing tranquility in the men—with what accurately measured interval fell those cruel words:

"Company!...Attention!...Shoulder arms!...Ready!...Aim!...Fire!"

Farquhar dived—dived as deeply as he could. The water roared in his ears like the voice of Niagara, yet he heard the dull thunder of the volley and, rising again toward the surface, met shining bits of metal, singularly flattened, oscillating slowly downward. Some of them touched him on the face and hands, then fell away, continuing their descent. One lodged between his collar and neck; it was uncomfortably warm and he snatched it out.

As he rose to the surface, gasping for breath, he saw that he had been a long time under water; he was perceptibly farther downstream—nearer to safety. The soldiers had almost finished reloading; the metal ramrods flashed all at once in the sunshine as they were drawn from the barrels, turned in the air, and thrust into their sockets. The two sentinels fired again, independently and ineffectually.

The hunted man saw all this over his shoulder; he was now swimming vigorously with the current. His brain was as energetic as his arms and legs; he thought with the rapidity of lightning:

"The officer," he reasoned, "will not make that martinet's error a second time. It is as easy to dodge a volley as a single shot. He has probably already given the command to fire at will. God help me, I cannot dodge them all!"

An appalling splash within two yards of him was followed by a loud, rushing sound, DIMINUENDO, which seemed to travel back through the air to the fort and died in an explosion which stirred the very river to its deeps! A rising sheet of water curved over him, fell down upon him, blinded him, strangled him! The cannon had taken an hand in the game. As he shook his head free from the commotion of the smitten water he heard the deflected shot humming through the air ahead, and in an instant it was cracking and smashing the branches in the forest beyond.

"They will not do that again," he thought; "the next time they will use a charge of grape. I must keep my eye upon the gun; the smoke will apprise me—the report arrives too late; it lags behind the missile. That is a good gun."

Suddenly he felt himself whirled round and round—spinning like a top. The water, the banks, the forests, the now distant bridge, fort and men, all were commingled and blurred. Objects were represented by their colors only; circular horizontal streaks of color—that was all he saw. He had been caught in a vortex and was being whirled on with a velocity of advance and gyration that made him giddy and sick. In few moments he was flung upon the gravel at the foot of the left bank of the stream—the southern bank—and behind a projecting point which concealed him from his enemies. The sudden arrest of his motion, the abrasion of one of his hands on the gravel, restored him, and he wept with delight. He dug his fingers into the sand, threw it over himself in handfuls and audibly blessed it. It looked like diamonds, rubies, emeralds; he could think of nothing beautiful which it did not resemble. The trees upon the bank were giant garden plants; he noted a definite order in their arrangement, inhaled the fragrance of their blooms. A strange roseate light shone through the spaces among their trunks and the wind made in their branches the music of Aeolian harps. He had not wish to perfect his escape—he was content to remain in that enchanting spot until retaken.

A whiz and a rattle of grapeshot among the branches high above his head roused him from his dream. The baffled cannoneer had fired him a random farewell. He sprang to his feet, rushed up the sloping bank, and plunged into the forest.

All that day he traveled, laying his course by the rounding sun. The forest seemed interminable; nowhere did he discover a break in it, not even a woodman's road. He had not known that he lived in so wild a region. There was something uncanny in the revelation.

By nightfall he was fatigued, footsore, famished. The thought of his wife and children urged him on. At last he found a road which led him in what he knew to be the right direction. It was as wide and straight as a city street, yet it seemed untraveled. No fields bordered it, no dwelling anywhere. Not so much as the barking of a dog suggested human habitation. The black bodies of the trees formed a straight wall on both sides, terminating on the horizon in a point, like a diagram in a lesson in perspective. Overhead, as he looked up through this rift in the wood, shone great golden stars looking unfamiliar and grouped in strange constellations. He was sure they were arranged in some order which had a secret and malign significance. The wood on either side was full of singular noises, among which—once, twice, and again—he distinctly heard whispers in an unknown tongue.

His neck was in pain and lifting his hand to it found it horribly swollen. He knew that it had a circle of black where the rope had bruised it. His eyes felt congested; he could no longer close them. His tongue was swollen with thirst; he relieved its fever by thrusting it forward from between his teeth into the cold air. How softly the turf had carpeted the untraveled avenue—he could no longer feel the roadway beneath his feet!

Doubtless, despite his suffering, he had fallen asleep while walking, for now he sees another scene—perhaps he has merely recovered from a delirium. He stands at the gate of his own home. All is as he left it, and all bright and beautiful in the morning sunshine. He must have traveled the entire night. As he pushes open the gate and passes up the wide white walk, he sees a flutter of female garments; his wife, looking fresh and cool and sweet, steps down from the veranda to meet him. At the bottom of the steps she stands waiting, with a smile of ineffable joy, an attitude of matchless grace and dignity. Ah, how beautiful she is! He springs forwards with extended arms. As he is about to clasp her he feels a stunning blow upon the back of the neck; a blinding white light blazes all about him with a sound like the shock of a cannon—then all is darkness and silence!

Peyton Farquhar was dead; his body, with a broken neck, swung gently from side to side beneath the timbers of the Owl Creek bridge.

Hank Lazer

N27P5

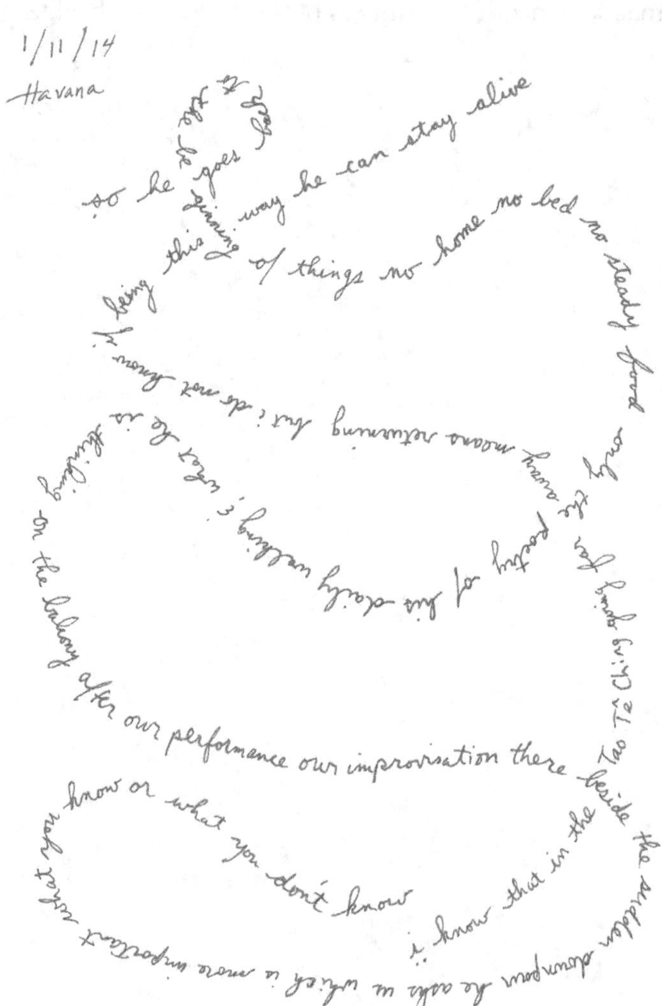

Hank Lazer

N27P9

1/12/14
Havana

(it was said to me
& i say it to you)

do not listen
as a trained musician
listen to what you are seeing here until what you are seeing becomes a music & a rhythm & a beginning set of sounds & a way to listen & become the music of a beckoned listening

"language does not presuppose thought, it accomplishes thought." [182]

for ARD

Hank Lazer

N27P10

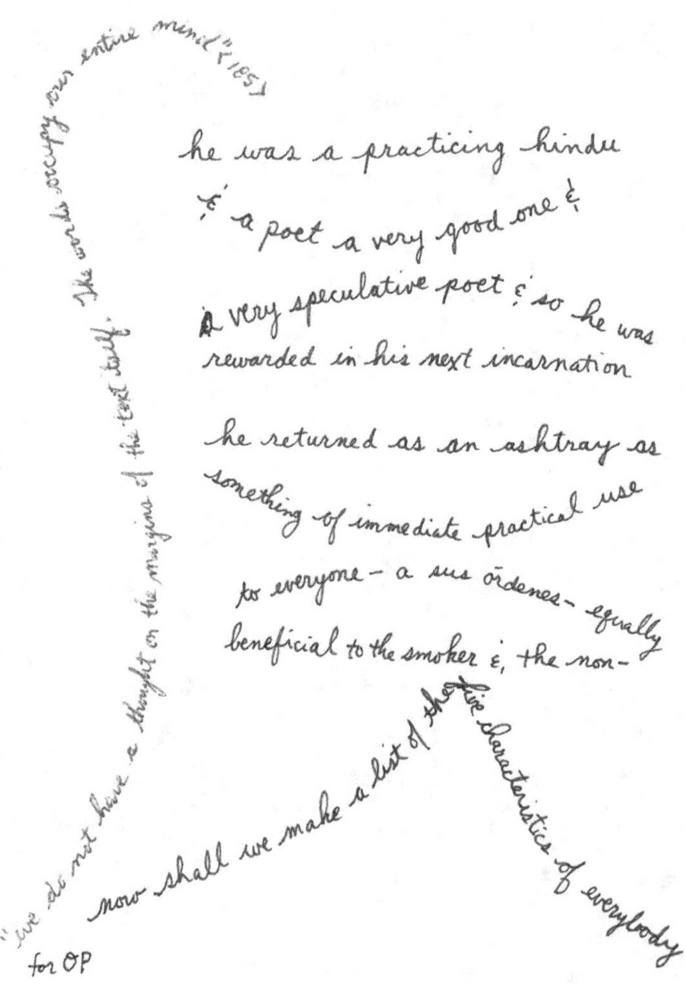

"we do not have a thought on the margins of the text itself. The words occupy our entire mind" & 1857

he was a practicing hindu
& a poet a very good one &
a very speculative poet & so he was
rewarded in his next incarnation

he returned as an ashtray as
something of immediate practical use

to everyone – a sus órdenes – equally
beneficial to the smoker & the non-

now shall we make a list of the five characteristics of everybody

for OP

Hank Lazer

N27P22

2/2/14

"Speech is the excess of our existence beyond natural being." <203>

mark plain as day can it be read a washing off

or the typical rain sound of random grayness

remarkable where to turn or what turn toward or into particular set of words

we are running out of time decomposing & indistinguishable from it

what would it be irregular rhythm music of this imperceptible falling into

"I have no other means of knowing the human body than by living it, that is, by taking up for myself the drama that moves through it and by merging with it." <205>

"Obscurity spreads to the perceived world in its entirety." <205>

Jesse Lee Wooton

AN UNCTION FROM THE HOLY ONE

The sign at the county line said Crow County. The first exit off of Interstate 65 was for Scotsville, and the second was for Athens. Scotsville was the county seat, and home to most of the business in the county. Four miles of empty road and pulp wood separated the two little towns, and it was nothing to see someone you knew walking between them. Most would refuse a ride if you offered—not that they didn't appreciate it, but walking was good for you, and laziness was a sin. People in the surrounding counties called the place Little Kentucky, because almost all the people who lived there were transplants from Perry, Leslie, Knott, or Preston County. They had come north to Indiana looking for work in the fifties and stayed—American Can and Cummins Diesel had good benefits and retirement if you weren't afraid to work hard. Most weren't, and prospered.

Those who didn't call it Little Kentucky called it Stinktown, because of the runoff of sludge from the canning factory, and the four foot deep trenches at the sides of the roads that the city sewage drained into. It was bad in winter, and unbearable in summer, but you got used to it.

Somebody made the comment once that a bag of unknown seed had been spilled in Crow County, and had come up churches. There was literally one on every corner in both Athens and Scotsville, and many more out in the county at wide places beside the road where somebody had donated land or a group of believers had pooled their money and bought a couple of lots meant for a business. There was one Church of Christ, and one Baptist—the rest were variations on Pentecostal faith.

There was the House of Prayer, and the Trinity House of Prayer. There was the Church of God, the Church of God of Prophecy, the Church of The Living God, the Pentecostal Church of God, and the Church of God in Jesus' Name. There was the Church of The Lord Jesus Christ, the Apostolic Church of The Lord Jesus Christ, the Church of Jesus Christ With Signs and Wonders Following, and the Full Gospel Church Of The Lord Jesus Christ. There was the Pillar of Truth, the Word of Faith, and the Four Square Gospel. There was Free Pentecostal and Holiness. Every spring the Lord sent somebody to set up a tent in the big field out by the interstate and hold revival as long as the people could stand it, and people from all the churches in the county came every night that their own home church didn't meet. It was easy and there was little conflict, because all these churches believed almost exactly the same thing.

Some permitted their members to smoke.

Some permitted the women to wear pants.

Some permitted the women to braid their hair.

Some permitted the women to wear jewelry.

Some permitted the men to wear short sleeves.

All of them agreed that it was a sin for a woman to cut her hair, but each had a different explanation for why. Understanding why something was a sin was part of the blessing that comes from knowing the truth and being closer to God than the others. They might all still be saved, but still, they weren't saved like we were.

The sign in front of the church in the middle of the block, on Broadway between US 31 and Mann Avenue, read Independent Interdenominational Free Pentecostal Church Of The Holy Ghost. The members had no idea what Interdenominational meant, but it looked good and they had been denied credentials from every other organization in the area. Both Churches of God, of Anderson, Indiana and the Cleveland, Tennessee Assembly, had sent memos to their state overseers to take note of this church. They were the kind who proudly called themselves "holy rollers" and gave people of faith a bad name in the conservative secular world which was sometimes the church's ally in political matters.

The pastor, Elhannon "Buster" Jones and his assistant, Brother Harvey Madden, had led the congregation without schism or ism for fifteen years. They had not differed in word, deed, or doctrine since the day Buster took over for Brother Ford Caudill, who had grown too old to stand unaided behind the pulpit and decided that it was just good wisdom to let the younger generation have a shot at being God's stewards. Some of the members had felt that the roles should have been reversed, putting Brother Harvey in the position of greater authority, but Harvey had never once voiced discontentment with Brother Ford's decision. The two men seemed to work perfectly together, like the varied and sundry parts of a well made watch.

Until the business with the hat.

The Bible said that any man praying or prophesying having his head covered, dishonored his own head. In spite of this, Buster had started to dream of standing in the pulpit, on fire for God, preaching the greatest message of his life, anointed of the Lord and overcome with the Glory, wearing the ball cap he had been given when he test drove a new Chevrolet Impala at Lewis Motors in Cruthersville. After the third time he had the dream, Buster went to Velocity Market on 256 and brought back a medium sized bottle of Pompei Virgin Olive Oil and poured the whole thing over the hat, praying that God would give him the interpretation of this dream. Anointed with oil, and the spirit, this hat meant something he didn't yet understand, but would, in God's good time. Yes, in God's good time. Everything would soon be made clear.

Buster's wife Arkie didn't question him when he told her not to move the hat from the corner of the dresser where he kept it. He told her that the hat was important somehow, he didn't know exactly how yet, but the Lord had showed him in a dream that there was something special about this particular hat.

While Buster was gone to work that day she prayed with the hat, standing beside the dresser with her hands outstretched, eyes closed. As she prayed, the Lord reminded her of the story of Elijah and Elisha, and how when Elijah's mantle fell from the chariot of fire, it was taken up by Elisha, who received a double portion of the spirit that blessed Elijah. Cold chills ran up and down her spine, and she felt the Holy Ghost running through her body like an electric current. She wept with joy at the prospect of her household being blessed that way—the man God had given her to as a help mate would soon be blessed beyond what any of them had ever experienced before. Her feet barely touched the floor as she went about her day's work. The greatest blessing of their lives was coming. She could almost see the Glory Of God shining through the house as she cleaned.

That evening when he got home from work, Buster went into the bedroom and prayed for guidance. The hat fairly hummed with energy as he knelt beside the bed. The sensation was so strong that he began to feel a presence in the room with him, intruding upon his prayers. He knew that nothing of God would interfere with his supplications, so whatever this was, must not be actually disrupting him, but must be part of God's plan. Angels were God's messengers on Earth. Buster realized that there was an angel in the room with him, perhaps even Michael or Gabriel, there in the humble room where he had laid his head in peaceful, blessed sleep all this time. He did not look up or around—he felt the bright glory of such a thing might daze him, and make him falter. Buster bowed his head lower, and the hair on the back of his neck rose and bristled as he felt hands on his shoulders, strong and firm, yet amazingly gentle. A steady stream of tears rolled off his cheeks as he felt God's personal messenger place the ball cap on his head. His chin shuddered and his lips formed words he did not know. Wings surrounded him and he felt himself carried away, as he knew he one day would be in the Rapture, and his voice broke because he could not contain the joy he felt as he heard a sound that could only be the golden crowns of four and twenty elders cast onto the floor in front of God's throne, and the last thing he remembered was their voices crying HOLY, HOLY, HOLY, for all eternity.

The chenille bedspread was wet with Buster's tears. A single drop of blood stained the white, and it reminded him of the blood of the lamb, who gave his life so that the whole world might be saved. Buster thought about Jesus praying in the garden, when he prayed so hard he sweated blood, and thought that might have been what he had done. Really, he had bitten his lip, and wouldn't realize it until Arkie made barbecued chicken for supper and the sauce stung the sore spot inside his mouth.

Sunday night after service was over and the congregation was gone, Buster told Brother Harvey about his experiences. He told the assistant pastor that he believed the Lord wanted him to preach a message wearing that hat. He told Harvey that if they obeyed the Lord just right, the whole house would be blessed greater than anything they had ever imagined. Eye hath not seen, neither hath ear heard. Buster was shocked that Harvey didn't take to the idea right away.

"Brother, if you had seen as I did," Buster said.

"Brother Buster, I'd have to be led direct of the Lord myself to go along with such a thing," Harvey said. "It contradicts the scripture. That's a hard thing."

The two of them sat on the altar and prayed. Buster prayed that God would reveal things to Brother Harvey as He had to him.

Harvey prayed that God would move on Brother Buster's life so that he could see the error of his thinking and forget about this hat foolishness. If it persisted, he'd have to call for a vote among the membership to remove the pastor and install somebody new. Somebody not so easily led astray, cast about by every wind of doctrine.

Every night that week, Harvey prayed for his pastor.

Buster worked nights in his garage building a box to house the anointed hat. His first idea was a simple cube, plain all around with no adornment at all. He gave up on that after dreaming about the children of Israel marching through the desert with the Ark that held the Ten

Commandments.

Buster would build one to hold his anointed ball cap.

Something so sacred needed to be carried in something special.

Buster and Arkie would carry the Ark into the church as the Levite priests had carried God's word and place it on the altar. He would open it in front of the congregation and let them see what God had placed such importance upon. Once they saw, he knew that his brothers and sisters, who shared the same spirit that he partook of, would see that this was of God, and would rejoice in the blessing that would be theirs because he had obeyed the Lord.

Harvey Madden was about to have none of this, and would do whatever it took to see that God's Holy Temple was not profaned.

Buster was reminded of John the Baptist preparing the way before Jesus began his ministry. Even when something came directly from God himself, people had to be led to it slowly, eased into new things. The shock of revelation was too much for some people's system to handle. You had to give a baby milk before the meat.

At the next service, Buster and Arkie carried the walnut box into the sanctuary, and put it on a table before the altar. When people asked what it was for, Buster would tell the inquisitive brother or sister to pray, and inquire of the Lord whether or not it was of Him. Buster asked Harvey not to tell anybody about what they had discussed. If anybody had anything to say on the subject that contradicted what Buster knew to be true, let them bring it to him without prompting or coaching. If it was revealed, without anybody who already knew letting it out, then Buster would have to consider the subject more closely. And if he was wrong, he would accept his rebuke with all the humility due. Buster decided that if he was that far wrong, on this or any other matter, he would step down and hand the reigns of the church over to Harvey, and would no more call himself a minister of God. He would be a saint, and no more.

But he wasn't worried. He knew he was right, and the only comments the box would generate would be a string of wrong guesses about what it contained. When confronted with such things, he would tell the speaker to stop guessing and pray.

During the next few services, Buster would pause between the opening song and the prayer requests and tie a red bandanna around his head. He would stand there with his eyes closed for just a minute, then swipe the thing off his head and put it in his front pocket without comment. The one time anybody asked him what he was doing, he pointed at the box next to the altar and said, "Pray." A few of the people he had said this to misunderstood and dropped to their knees on the spot. Some thought he was telling them to pray to the box.

Word began to spread that Brother Buster had lost the goods, and was suggesting that people make wooden idols and pray to them.

It was Brother Keith Coldiron that put that story to rest. He told people that the box held two live rattlesnakes, and one service soon, Buster was going to bring them out and tell people the Lord had commanded him to "take up the serpent."

"I know that's what it is," Brother Keith said." I put my ear against the box last week and heard 'em rattling and singing in there. When he does, you'll not find Brother Coldiron amongst the congregation no more. I'll shake the dust off my feet for a testimony against the place." He shook his head in disgust. It had been his home church since the day he repented the first time after the police took him to jail for stealing Marty Goodin's Farmall tractor. He'd feel strange anyplace else.

Brother Harvey did his best to assure that congregation that things were not as bad as they seemed. He told people that Brother Buster was "trying the spirits, to see whether or not they be of God," just as the Book commanded the prudent to do. "Whatsoever this strange thing may be, hold fast to the Lord, and listen to the still, small voice that has led you this far, and God as my witness you'll not go wrong." And that seemed to help.

Harvey thought about the story of the watchman on the watchtower, and how he let the enemy approach without giving sufficient warning. The blood of the innocent was on that man's hands. He had a responsibility he didn't live up to, and would wear the stain of his failure for all eternity, even if he found the grace to be forgiven enough to enter the Kingdom.

Harvey's robe of white would have no such blemishes.

Sometimes, in war, you got blood on you from the wounded around you. Sometimes soldiers were even killed by their own people.

They called it "friendly fire."

Whatever blood Brother Harvey got on him would come clean, when he was washed in the blood of the lamb.

And he would stand before God, blameless.

Harvey believed that the situation would come to a head during the regular Sunday Night Service. It was not a guess. It was not prophecy. He believed that it was revelation, direct from the Great White Throne, as certain as that given to Saint John and recorded in the last book of the Bible. There were no visions or dreams, and it was not spoken of, but he felt it was true.

And so it was.

The last Sunday Night Service in September started the usual way. The minstrels played and sang, and every mind in the house came into one accord.

Ike Stidham sang, "That's Why We Baptize In Jesus' Name."

Marty Howard sang, "God's Not Dead."

Eli Ritchie sang, "Ain't No Grave."

The sisters of the church came together and sang, "My Mind's Made Up."

All during the singing, Buster kept looking at the walnut box on the table beside the altar. Harvey noticed and kept watching Buster.

Buster nodded to Harvey, his signal to take prayer requests. A half dozen stood and gave spoken requests, and then Harvey asked for raised hands to signal unspoken requests. The entire congregation knelt, and Harvey prayed that this cup pass from him, if it might be within the Lord's will. He felt no guidance on the subject as he prayed, and comforted himself by putting his hand in the right pocket of the light jacket he wore. As the crowd turned and took their seats, Buster walked to the front of the altar and opened the wooden box there. All eyes were on Buster as he opened the lid. The front was attached to the bottom with hinges so that it could be lowered to display the contents. Buster stood to one side and allowed everyone to see.

"There's been a lot of talk about what I've had hid in this box," Buster said. "I never meant for it to be no big secret, but this is something the Lord has put on my heart, and the time has come to share it with you." He put his left hand on his chest, as if saying the Pledge to the Flag. His right hand hovered over the polyester ball cap in the box. "The Lord has put a special anointing on this hat, and intends for me to give the message wearing it. I know what the book says, and they's such a thing as rightly dividing the word of truth. All I'm gonna do is obey the Lord as best as I know how, and ask you all to pray for me. If you find fault with what I do, pray and ask the Lord to show you what he's showed me." Buster picked up the hat and held it before him. He turned it side to side, as if examining some rare find, then lowered it so those in the front pew could see up close. The oil Buster had rubbed on it had soured and turned brown, and those close enough to smell it turned away. Harvey walked up behind Buster and put his hand on the pastor's shoulder.

Buster put the hat back in the box and turned to face the man who had stood by and supported him in his ministry since the day they had opened the doors to the place. Harvey whispered something in Buster's ear that the rest couldn't hear, then went back and took his usual seat. Buster dropped his head and closed his eyes. He prayed for strength. Harvey did the same.

What Harvey whispered to Buster was, "It ain't gonna happen."

Buster took his usual place behind the altar and said, loud enough to be heard in the parking lot, "I'm gonna obey the Lord, if it harelips everything from here to Indianapolis."

He said, "As children of God, we are in the world, but not of the world."

He said, "The children of God are a peculiar people."

He said, "According to the word, we are to lean not to our own understanding."

He said, "I will not lean to my own understanding. I will listen to the still, small voice that speaks to me, the same still, small voice that spoke to Samuel in the house of Eli, the same still, small voice that spoke to Moses in the burning bush, the same still, small voice that spoke to Paul on the road to Damascus." Buster began to pace back and forth behind the altar. At each end he spun around like a lawyer pointing out the guilty party among the spectators at a trial.

He stopped at the lectern and gripped the sides. He said, "I will HEED the voice of the GOD of ALL CREATION who spoke the world into existence, and I will KEEP the covenant our fathers have made with HIM. The same GOD who said that DISOBEDIENCE is as the sin of WITCHCRAFT, and commanded his people under that law that they should not SUFFER A WITCH TO LIVE." Buster walked around to the front of the altar and took the ball cap from the box on the table. He snatched it up quickly, as if afraid if might move out of his grasp and if that happened he would never have the chance to obey God this way again. He knew that God would give his children every chance he could, just as he did Jonah who sought to escape his duty, but once that mercy was exhausted, there would be no more chances. Buster Jones was not a man to try the patience of God. He held the cap up in front of the congregation and said, "BEHOLD, I SHOW YOU A MYSTERY!" and placed the cap on his head as if it were the crown that the prophet placed on Saul's head when he became the first king of Israel. Buster splayed his arms out, transfixed, transfigured, transformed. He felt the white light of The Savior's Glory surrounding him, changing him, healing him. He felt the hand of God as His palm pressed against the back of his head. Then he felt nothing.

"Blasphemer!" shouted Harvey. No one heard this, because Harvey's voice was drowned out by the flat blat sound picked up by the microphone in Buster's hand, starting feedback in the amplifiers. It peaked with a high pitched whine, and then the house was silent. Buster was still on his feet, leaning forward at an odd angle, as if his chin rested on an invisible shelf. Harvey did not lower the hand that held the pistol till Buster fell to his knees. When Buster finally dropped, face down on the linoleum, his chin hit the floor at the exact same moment as Harvey's pistol. The "chunk" sound that everyone heard could have been either one.

The house erupted as people fought to be the first out the door. There was wailing, and gnashing of teeth, as tears blinded eyes and whispers of "Lord God Almighty" mingled with cries of "Jesus God, Jesus God." Marty Howard elbowed Sister Rosetta Stidham in the ear and knocked her down as he stepped on her mother's back getting out the door. Most, once they made it outside, kept walking, some leaving behind their cars and walking alongside the road with no destination in mind other than "away from here." Some got in their cars and locked the doors. Some stood at the edge of the parking lot and tried to look back inside, as if that much distance was all the safety they needed. A few prayed. A few gathered into small groups and tried to figure out what they had seen. Half an hour passed before anybody thought to call the police. Arkie Jones called the television station in Louisville, and the pastor of the Church of God Cleveland, Tennessee Assembly.

The next day it was said that Harvey blew Buster's head off with a shot gun. Hazel Cattlett said her granny came home from church with a piece of Buster's brains in her hair. It was said that the men fought before church, and Harvey threatened the pastor. Bonnie Johnson said Harvey had a black eye before hand. It was said that one of the deputies took home the Colt Python .357 Magnum that Harvey used, and was letting people shoot it down on the bank of the Muscatatuck River for five dollars a shot. This was partly true. He was charging people to shoot such a gun, but it was not the one Harvey had used. Harvey had killed Buster with a .22.

The congregation scattered and the church on Broadway closed. Members at their new churches would at first ask if they knew what happened. There were as many versions of the story as there were of Pentecostal doctrine. Depending on who you asked, Harvey was in the state prison at Michigan City, the psych hospital at Madison, or a halfway house in Sellersburg. More than a dozen of the sisters who were present later claimed to have been shown what was about to happen in a dream the night before. Opinions varied as to which of the two, Buster or Harvey, was in the right. Nobody from the church has yet said that neither was.

Brad Garber

DESERT NOTES

Slab stone embrace volcanic heat bodies
Cory's Special split horse teeth candles
Fire morning clouds bacon banana bread
\Howls hoots hollows Ford dumper ornament
Craft of ancients mule deer coyotes
Cow bones bleached deer barbed wire
Cattle lonely guarding limestone lintels
Settler walls of hope Franks Simon Harris
Owls barn great sage willow roof
Lone walker dawn camp coffee steaming
Tom Sandy Carl turkey oysters spaghetti
Whiskey road sex fossil soft beds down
Heavy sun eyes California quail eagles
Hamas Israeli cease guitar moon rings
Around waxing moon snake bodies twist
Thick colored wool rock birds burst
Lemon Jelly Zeppelin endless mirrors
Cave winter sunlight Doris fur boot helmet
Road dirt road plume hats hot bog pool
Power water trough lines light travel
Hoof rib blood bone shirtless roaring Ray
Regal bucks does low gear rock growl
Small bird hunters Eastern kingbirds blue
Birds around corpse truck hood liquor
Sparkles hillsides been everywhere Cash
Gates to Stairway Hell silent engines
Best biscuits made granite pipes pot
Jessy Steven camping feral mules
Unexpected generosity bog springs antelope
Country warm laughing fire night clouds
Last soak freedom long crooked twisting
Dust prints to peace

Rachel Jamison Webster

CHILD IN A SPHERE OF LIGHT,

—after Odilon Redon

1. Mother

The child's star is gathering force,
curving in the egg around her,
combs and cups of energy
she sits in to read or crochet,
quiet times she feels her mind
winging silver into the drifts
of the stars and has to thread
herself back to her hands—
how surprising they are!
Little linked wands of bone,
and whorls of skinridge,
even the dust on the sill
a thin descendant of them,
of the light drifting down
to her as if in readying.
Soon it will confront her
in form and they will enclose
each other in the heat
that poppies bloom from,
the eye that swims before the sun.

2. Child

The child is himself and not yet
mother, beholding the world
through its curve. Once you realize
nothing is wrong, then you see.
Now light is all he can be
amid the riffing repetitions,
where even breaking is all

he needs of beauty. It unravels
to a tined fraying,
a crown of the charge
we call meaning and so often
give away to some god.
He's at the age he could be
either a he or a she.
The gold around his face
is the blessing his parents gave,
while the white muscling up
is his very own being
and he knows this
fist, the small reptilian head
that will drink of the heart
to enlarge him. And the world
seen through his body's rim
(the world with its bluing drifts
and hot mottles of sun!)
will be as bright—no brighter—
than the eye it has sprung from.

Rachel Jamison Webster

ESTUARY

Those murmuring waves I was
so long beside were not stronger
than the voice of the future.
I heard that voice in his
like a current in a river,
mouthing the clear in clear
in galloping waters, wanting
those waters and the children
of those waters. I had known
only stones and watermouths
enfolding the stones to open
motion from a growing absence,
a rippling in rings rhymed
with eternity. This is not
eternity, but life we're stalking.
When a river enters a lake
both faces reverberate.

Rachel Jamison Webster

FIGHTING FEVER

She'll sleep only in my arms today,
cheeks flushed as fruit, hair wet in waves
across her brow as my thoughts
slosh and break around the little room.

A bear tiptoes across rooftops
soaked in yellow dawn.

Bluebirds sing from shirtfronts.

A girl in pigtails holds up a sun
on a stick, or is it a peach,
or is it her poem?

I rock us on an inky sea, a spiraling
rug braided by my grandma
when her hands were good

made of jeans my parents wore
when they were young and rocking me.

Outside black-eyed Susans nod in noon.
Gulls V, then careen and wing
apart. She's past the rocky cliff

of sleep now, she's loosened her clasp
of my hand, her hand just loosening
its baby stitch of dimples.

Someday I will read this poem
and try to remember the smell of her sleep,
the fan beating like a third, timekeeping heart,
noonlight strained through dotted Swiss,

and why I extracted myself and laid her down
to write this.

Brian L. Tucker

CLIMBING ABOVE GROUND

Tracey went back to a school that wasn't there, kicked around some left-over bricks. A few cars looked to be cemented to the abandoned parking lot. A bus with kudzu exploding from its hood. The sign that once gave this place a name boldly proclaiming *Seton Independent School*, now fragmented, simply read *ton pendent hool.*

No one was around. Tracey side-armed a limestone pebble in her anger, and looked above the buildings to see if the old, rock quarry was still there. She remembered trucks once hauled rocks from point A to B.

The *hool,* or school, whatever one preferred, used to be a majestic place—with snotty-nosed kids. The schoolhouse was one of those K through 12 scenarios, where seniors knew second-graders. Tracey remembered being voted "best all-around" her senior year. The prize ultimately went to Dixie Dodson; she settled for "most likely to succeed."

That same year, complete with a backpack, a fancy notebook, and a lot of beef jerky, Tracey left the familiar foothills and ventured to Harrow State University. She'd studied law and graduated at the top.

Today, was her triumphant return home. Her ten-year reunion; her chance to finally prove herself worthy of a never-bestowed, senior title.

The only problem: there wasn't a high school on Hill Street anymore.

The demolition crew took the frame down a week prior. She didn't know anybody's phone number, and their class president, Stanley Boggs, was responsible for planning the reunion. Tracey tried to email Boggs, but the result was null. *He always had been too cool.*

Tracey imagined she would be the only attendee "flying solo" at her reunion, when, or if, it happened. She searched her car for a ponytail holder. When she found one, she twisted the band firmly into place. Tracey thought, *Forget this*, and resigned to leave a note on one of the abandoned cars.

She scribbled with a half-used, Pentel fountain pen:

"Tracey Sharpe, Class of '03. Trying to connect for SHS reunion, 602-8503. *Thanks."*

She lifted a Jeep Grand Cherokee's wiper, tucked the note against the windshield. It looked the least abandoned of any car in the lot. Feeling that initial surge of hope, she locked her car and commenced walking the old, school grounds.

The word *rubble* came to her mind, as she moved clockwise around the vacant lot. There were a few recognizable relics from the past. Tracey remembered "Field Day" in primary school. This particular patch of schoolyard where she'd taken the lead in a race—beaten the class bully, Sammy Tangler. Suddenly, a person yelled from where the tech ed classroom once stood.

She couldn't make out what they wanted, and yelled back, "Can I help you Mr...?"

"Nickson. Is that you? Tracey, dear?"

"Do I know you? Forgive me."

"Nonsense. You know it's been a while for both of us. I was a teacher in fourth grade. You had my colleague, Ms. Montoya."

Images of recess and geography quizzes came rushing back at the mention of Ms. Montoya. "What're you doing here?"

"Trying to move some of these pieces of the gym flooring. See them? These were left here from the court you once played balled on. Help me out and you can take some with you."

Tracey saw the floor pieces, something she'd missed earlier, and reached down and started rubbing the smooth pieces of hardwood flooring. They looked like jigsaw pieces when held together. Abandoned and in disrepair.

"You were quite the little scrapper on the courts, I remember," Mr. Nickson said. "You got better in high school, too. How did college work out to...where was it?"

"Harrow State."

"Yes. You went on a ball scholarship, right? But, got there and decided to go pre-law. Is what your mom said."

Tracey put the wooden planks in a pile mimicking Mr. Nickson and stood back, admiring the aging man. "You sure do know me still."

"My job," he laughed. "Once a crazy teacher. Always a crazy one. Besides, you made all of us proud around here."

Tracey felt herself blush; she wanted to ask him a million questions but realized he looked in a hurry to get somewhere. He scooped up an armful of planks and nodded towards the Jeep. She cleared her throat. "So, that's *my* note on your windshield. In case, you're wondering who the "other" crazy person is. You don't have to answer that cry for help, if you don't want."

"Geez, I would Tracey, but I told some other teachers I'd be bringing these boards to them in town today. They were especially excited to hear that these hadn't burned up or been destroyed...yet."

"Why would someone do that to Seton High?" she blurted out, not meaning to.

"I want to help with your class' reunion. Really. Will you be here for a little while?" he asked, his cloudy, blue eyes trying to see into hers, ignoring her question.

She remembered his polite tone, even back in fourth grade when no one warranted patience. She nodded, "I don't have anywhere else I'm expected to be. It'd mean a lot."

He said he'd be back and pulled out of the school parking lot slowly. A tattered *Go Lions* sticker still clinging to his bumper.

Tracey went back to the remains of the old, tech ed classroom. Then, she peered around to where the school swimming pool once held water. Now, it was just a mound of debris. The bunker, where a cement cavity rested, now acted as a giant sarcophagus for antiquated, Apple computers. There were hundreds of desktop frames rammed into this single concrete shell. She kicked a hard drive for sport and watched a mound of frames topple over into the pool. It made a loud racket. *Too loud.* Tracey walked around Hill Street's deserted intersection—to see if anyone else noticed.

Emptiness filled the street. No traffic in either direction.

Tracey remembered swimming laps in the dimly lit arena. *It really was one-of-a-kind.* It was Olympic-sized and looked like something a person would see at the Biltmore Estate. The stinging sensation of water burning her nostrils was as present now as it'd been when Mr. Wilcox threw her head first into the water at a middle school swim meet, and yelled, "Catch em, girl!"

Beyond the swimming pool was where the marching band practiced, the outdoor clay courts. She'd participated in impromptu games of kickball and freeze tag; she even remembered holding hands with her first crush, Benny Morris. His hands had been softer than hers, somehow, and the thought now repulsed her.

Only the concrete wall remained. A place where those "going steady" kissed when teachers were distracted by "mock" fistfights. Tracey smiled at the notion of kissing in such a public place as this. She remembered the concrete wall always cold to the touch—on the back of one's legs especially.

"Can I help you, young lady?" a man asked, wearing a jumpsuit.

"It's Miss Sharpe," she said. "And, no. I'm just looking around...at the *progress*. I must say it's coming along." She dusted her hands off in a sign of business-like approval.

"Progress?" the man asked. "Not the word I'd use exactly," and he pointed at the jackhammered courts.

The playground was no longer a place for four-square and hop-scotch. It'd become a desolate and destitute area, where weeds grew quickly through the cracks.

"The whole thing is just waiting to be sucked under by the cave system you know? One small tectonic shift and the whole darn thing is going under. We might end up really down under, if we're lucky. Wouldn't that be nice, *mate*?" He mimicked a terrible, Australian accent.

Tracey laughed and asked why he wore a jumpsuit like he was in prison or something. She realized this question would've normally shocked her—just out with it. But, college *had* developed forthrightness in her.

"I *am* in prison," he replied matter-of-factly, looking her squarely in the eyes.

"Ohh," Tracey stammered. "That's nice. Which one?" knowing there was only one in Seton, Kentucky.

"Cumberland."

"And you're...doing what?"

"I work on *this* heap each day until they tell me to stop," the man pointed to all of the rubble which was back-dropped behind them. He flipped the bird at an overseer Tracey hadn't spotted earlier who held a rifle and waved it sternly over at him and Tracey. The prisoner told her to be careful. This place was filled with spots just waiting to go under... beyond...down to Chinatown.

She said she would, walked quickly away from him and the man with the gun.

Past the courts she stopped in a small field, where all of the dangerous—and since then, outlawed—pieces of rusted metal equipment rested for eternity. It was what Tracey called: *Willy Wonka Wonderland*. It all sat on the backside of the Seton Independent school system.

When the recess bell dinged, she remembered being the first outside. Explorer of a new toy each and every fourth grade day. First, she'd ran to the monkey bars. These were a spin on the traditional version, she remembered. They were elevated about three feet higher than the standard ones. The swings and monkey bars were now rusted almost completely in two. From their looks, a strong wind would be able to finish the job.

Then, she saw something else, and the memory took her breath away. *It* was still there and had been ever since her mom was a student—a metal ladder straight up towards heaven.

Like the Babylonians and their doomed stairway, this was constructed by someone—initially to bring joy to others. Tracey wasn't sure—and never had been sure—of who signed off on a design like this, but she remembered loving "the ladder." It went straight up two-and-a-half stories. The wind whistled through its rungs like a giant Cyclops humming a lullaby. The rust gave the once strong stairway a callused, penetrable look. It was ominous standing where a once well-known, country school educated so many. Tracey shook her head, walked over to the ladder. She put her hand on the second-to-bottom rung and peered at the top. It swayed a little in the gentle breeze.

She heard, "I wouldn't give that a go, if I were you, Miss Sharpe," from the direction of the prisoner crew. Then a different voice, "Keep at it, Johnson. I'd hate to have to put the metal bracelets back on your wrists so soon."

She turned, saw the gun-guard barking more orders. Noticed that the prisoner who'd spoken to her was one of several men forced to jackhammer the play court into pieces—including all of its memories. For some reason, Tracey caught herself awkwardly mid-wave, waving in the direction of the men.

She decided to plan her ten-year reunion for a school that would only, and always, exist in her mind. She figured Mr. Nickson would be her guide anyways.

The sound of jackhammers shook the cave system below; it was the biggest cave in the country, she thought. Stalactites. Stalagmites. Speleothems. Any and all of those rock specimens were somewhere beneath her. The beauty of such rocks just below the rubble and dust at her feet.

Tracey walked back to see if the Jeep had returned. The schoolyard was one of the only things she still knew in Seton, and it was suddenly as lonely as a cave.

Dallas Fletcher

UNALOUD

There are just some things a boy does not naturally know: so, he is not sure what to do the moment the baby belches and white cream oozes from her mouth, slides down her chin, like a boat slowly moving along a river. If her mother, that girl, was carrying a diaper bag, she must have taken it in the house with her. He holds the baby out with one hand, gripping perhaps a little too hard, trying to make sure he doesn't drop her. Searching, he half-watches the drool slide towards the tip of her chin, all clotted and bubbly, and now he can smell it too as he reaches with the other hand through the window of his truck. Fumbling, he pulls on the knob of the glove compartment and finally feels it click. An avalanche of manuals and ketchup packets falls to the floor; he feels what he thinks is a napkin and pulls it out. In the bright light of the sweltering, swampy Alabama afternoon, he can see it's actually an old parking ticket, but it will have to do. He wipes her chin as best he can as she worms in his arm, trying to pull her head away from the rough paper. There is something soft about her even as she struggles; he realizes the girl never told him the baby's name, and so he whispers to her soft names that come to mind to see if she will respond: Anna, Grace. Brett. Hello, *Brett.*

But *Brett* is not such a soft name. He shifts his body, feeling the sleek carriage of the truck against his back, still warm from his four-hour drive from Savannah, and thinks of Brett from Hemingway's *The Sun Also Rises*. He fell in love with her in eleventh grade, even dropped German in favor of Spanish so one day he could move to Pamplona and become a bullfighter and meet someone like Brett who would be impressed with the way he could bring a *toro* to shame. But: in the back of his mind he always knew that Brett was dangerous, with her short hair and strong bones and the way she could leave a man crying in his bed at night. Though he was mesmerized by Brett he was, he realized now, scared by her too. Even so, he reread *The Sun* three times that summer, lying in his shorts against the cool sheets at night with a flashlight, imagining Brett snuggled up against him, his heart beating fast in his chest.

Something brushes against his leg and he lets out a startled dog-yelp. The baby squeals too, a big grin on her face, and he trips over his own feet as he hops sideways away from the truck, his heart racing to catch back up after a sudden instant of not beating. The sides of his shoes stir up lonesome clouds of red dust from the grassless yard. A fat chicken with feathers the color of pancake syrup shuffles out from under the truck. She turns her beady eyes towards him, the pouch under her chin bloating in and out. He feels the baby bouncing, her fists thumping against his arm. Just a chicken. What was it Hemingway said about chickens?

Henrietta lets out a squawk, mocking him, and slowly starts to shuffle away. He takes a couple swaggers forward, slinging his foot out to the side, shooing her away. As if she knows he is scared to get too close, she just waddles from side to side, pausing to pick at something in the dust. The baby giggles at this and he turns to her, raising one eyebrow. "So you think it's funny, Meredith? Huh?" She lets out a long sigh and lets her head full of damp caramel curls fall against his chest.

The girl was carrying the baby close to her when he saw them slide past his window on Highway 20, west of Atlanta near the state line, out in the middle of the sticks. He was hauling his stuff back from the dorm, at the end of the semester, to his mother's house in Huntsville, but he was not anxious to get there, to unload his clothes and furniture into his dimly lit and musty room. His eyes followed the shape of the girl on the side of the road, her arms wrapped around and her head down to protect the baby from the swarms of dust from passing semis. A deep purple backpack swayed loosely from her shoulders. He slowly pressed his foot against the brake and let the pick-up drift onto the shoulder. Gravel crunched underneath the tires. Watching her in the rearview mirror, he could see her slow down and glance up, taking hesitant steps. He decided it was probably best to let her come to him; he stuck his arm out the window and waved for her to come up. The air conditioner had zonked out months ago, so he always drove with the windows down, and whenever he went anywhere he would climb out of the truck with his hair sticking out in strange places. Looking at himself now, he licked his fingers and ran them through his hair a couple times and then finally gave up. She came up to the opposite side of the truck, cradling the baby against her chest and stood back about a yard, tipping her head to see inside.

He leaned over, sliding his books and empty fast food bags and guitar picks off the passenger seat. "Want a ride?"

She peered at him, trying to decide. "I don't bite," he said. He grinned a little, curling the side of his mouth up, and wondered if she was staring at his hair. Without the air gushing through the windows at him, the cab was beginning to get hot, already. A small bead of sweat ran down her forehead, tracing a line in her skin. He licked his dry mouth, said, "Where you headed?"

"Oh, just a couple miles down the road," she said softly, her lips barely moving as she looked at him. "I guess I can just walk." She pulled her chin in but didn't move.

"It's too hot for you and your baby to be out here," he said. She glanced down and ran one hand over the baby's limp curls, nodding just barely. "Hop in. It's not much cooler but at least I can get you there faster."

The baby's mother had short curls too, a little darker, but the same damp and lifeless in the sun. The girl shifted her eyes left and right, as if to make sure there would be no better options suddenly appearing over the hill or out of the brush along the side of the road. Then she took a step forward and he leaned across the seat, hooking the handle with two fingers and pushing the door gently open. She managed to twist her way onto the seat, stepping up, the baby still cradled in her arms. The baby blinked and her gaze rolled around the cabin until it finally rested on him and she puckered her lips a little. She was just staring and staring, her eyes big and blue and focused on him as the girl slid onto the seat and shut the door. His wrist was resting on the steering wheel and he watched the baby lay her head on the girl's shoulder, still staring up at him.

"Okay." The girl slid close to the door, her bony hand stretched out and resting near the handle. "I'll tell you when to turn," she said, looked over at him and he pulled down on the gear lever, casting a glance in the rearview mirror and then easing the truck back onto the road. The asphalt was *hot*; watery stripes appeared in dips and ridges ahead and then disappeared as they grew closer. The air that whipped through the truck and around their heads pulled the humidity away from their skin, and the steady hum started to lull the baby to sleep as he drove on. He had always been bad at conversation, especially with girls. He could feel his fingertips sweating against the sticky leather of the steering wheel as he tried to think of something to say.

She lifted her hand and rubbed it over the back of her neck. "What's your name?" she asked.

His heart started beating faster and he glanced down at one of the books on the seat between them. "Holden," he said quickly and then looked out the side window, rolling his eyes. Why did he just say that?

"Well, thank you Holden." She leaned the baby back, resting the tiny head on her own outstretched knees that fit almost snug against the tan dashboard.

"You're welcome," he said, looking at her and then staring straight ahead.

From somewhere in the house comes the sound of glass breaking. The clapboard exterior had once been blue, he thinks, but most of the paint has been chipped away and even what is left is now a dingy gray. His mother's crazy aunt had a house like this; the cigar-shaped locusts that come swarming through Georgia and Alabama in the summer would crawl through the gaps in the walls, hungry and looking for food. If there is a clutch of bugs like that in this house, maybe it *is* better to keep the baby out here. "Huh, Tessa," he says to her, bouncing her up and down gently on the top of the truck. "Tessa?" She grins, showing a few teeth, and her eyes scan the yard. "Guess not," he says, hoisting her down and turning to see what she was looking at. Strutting and scratching its way across the dried clay, a cocky rooster with a head full of bright green feathers casually searches for some shade. Those chickens. How many are there? Maybe all these chickens eat the locusts before they make it into the house. Maybe they don't have to worry about that here.

He hears something heavy fall in the house and the sound of a male voice, tense and strained. Besides the gaps in the walls, the windows all the way around are open too. The same limp brown curtains hang in each window, unmoving against any small breezes that float through the yard. A horsefly buzzes around his ear and he swats at it, holding the baby against his ribcage with one arm. He wonders if summers in Spain are this hot.

"It's just up here," she said softly, motioning with her head. The baby was awake now with the swaying of the truck as it jostled over the tight dirt path. Striped shadows of overhanging sycamores rolled up and over the truck as they drove underneath. Ahead of him, a squirrel darted into the middle of the path and then back again, scattering two paws full of walnut shells in the dust.

"Kind of the middle of nowhere, huh?" he forced a small laugh and wiped his palm against his pant leg. The baby woke from the jostling of the truck, bouncing over ruts in the dry earth. She screeched, grabbing at the girl's sleeves and wriggling on her bare thighs. The baby turned and looked at him again and he wrinkled his face, sticking out his tongue. She laughed a little and the girl looked over at him, stared for a moment, and then pulled her baby close.

"Here it is." The dusty path spread out, leading into a whole yardful of dirt in front of a small house. "Oh, shit," she muttered.

"What?" He pressed on the brakes and the truck shuddered to a stop. He threw it into park and looked around. Sitting back under some trees, the branches draped with stringy Spanish moss like scattered dirty dishrags, were two cars, both old and rusty and cluttered with bumper stickers. She looked over at them and then down at the baby.

"Shit, oh, shit. What is *he* doing here?" She twitched, jerking the door open, and slid sideways out of the seat, glanced over her shoulder at the house and then pushed the baby across to him. The baby giggled and reached out, stretching, and clutched her tiny hands around a french fry box. "Holden, I'm so sorry. Can you? Just watch her a second. I'll be right out I swear." The girl backed up, biting her lip. She threw the purple bag over her shoulder and lunged her whole weight against the door as he blinked at her, leaning forward and smacking the dashboard.

"I don't—hey!"

The girl ran up to the house, the sun gleaming on her white calves. She opened the front door and let the screen slam shut behind her. His lips hung open, full of silent protests. The baby squealed beside him, rocking on her back. His books and papers beneath her crinkled. He turned off the truck and gazed down at her. She waved the fry box in her clutched hand and then looked at him upside-down with those big blue eyes. His fingers slowly uncurled from the key and he held his hand out above her for a moment, hovering, and then finally placed it gently on her stomach. It jiggled under his palm and he felt his heart slow down a little, her flesh and cotton t-shirt soft beneath his fingers.

"Hot in here, huh?" He pushed his door open, ran his hand through his disheveled hair, looking down at her, and then slipped his hand underneath, pulling her awkward weight against his chest and feeling her wet lips against his chin. Together they slid sideways out of the truck and stepped down into the dust.

The baby presses her feet against his stomach and stiffens her whole body, like a pulse of electricity has just surged through her. A sound like a baby pigeon's coo gurgles from her lips; she squirms, her arms wiggling and each roll of baby fat bouncing. He smiles down at her and thinks that they must both be bored. The girl has been in the house for almost a half hour and together he and the baby have walked to the treeline on the edge of the yard and back four times. She has held onto his fingers and squealed at the fat hen, has fussed at gnats in her ears and tapped her sticky fingers at her reflection in the side mirrors of the truck. Slowly, heavy cumulus clouds are spreading across the sky from the east and a random breeze laps at their skin just often enough to make them hungrier for it.

Another loud crash comes from the house and she quavers in his arms, startled. He hears a voice, a female voice, screaming, *fuck you, get off of me.* He cannot tell if it belongs to the girl, but the baby hears it and starts to whimper. A funny feeling slides into his stomach, and the heat turns it into a sudden nervous nausea. He stands in the dust, watching the house, listening, bouncing the baby in his arms.

"Shhh, Rosa..." Someday, when he is living the life of a bullfighter in Spain, he will have a housekeeper named Rosa who comes every Saturday to water the plants and place crisp new sheets on his bed. "Shhh, it's okay..." He rocks her softly back and forth in his arms, swaying from his waist, and looks at the house. Another loud thumping, a collapsing of something heavy comes through the windows and the female voice shrieks again, *goddamn piece of shit.* He takes a long breath to calm his stomach and moves closer to the house, listening, bouncing her up and down in his arms. "It's all right. Shhh." He rocks her back and forth in his arms as his legs trudge slowly forward.

There is a part, at the end of *The Sun Also Rises*, where Brett telegrams the hero and he drops everything to rescue her. Well, to come and get her, at least, and on those summer nights, dreaming about bullfights and late nights dancing to the music of drunken Spaniards, he imagined that he was the one holding the slip of paper, stretched tight between his thumbs and fingers.

✦

The baby wriggles aimlessly, flopping left and then right against his forearms. His dusty shoes trace the tire marks in the clay slowly towards the edge of the porch. Back in the shadows of the overhanging sycamores, the chickens are clucking, foraging for grubs under decaying branches.

The shouting inside crescendos, *mother-fucking, get the hell,* and then silence; he feels his heart racing and stares at the door, telling his feet to move. Move, move, go rescue. *COULD YOU COME HOTEL MONTANA MADRID AM RATHER IN TROUBLE BRETT.* His shoes refuse to budge and the baby coos, squirming. He feels a trickle of sweat sliding down his neck. The door flies open, clattering against the tired clapboard siding. She flies across the porch and down the steps without her backpack. Her face is red, her cheek an ugly purple. "We've got to go!" she shouts and jerks the baby from his arms. The baby starts to scream, holding her arms out and shaking them stiffly.

"Hey, be *careful* with her," he says. He stands half in and half out of the shadows.

"Holden! *Now!*" In one fluid movement she flings open the truck door, thrusts herself and the baby inside, slams them both in. He looks at her, hears something inside. The girl's eyes are wide through the windshield, her short damp curls flat against her scalp. The baby's lips move, open, wide and wet, but somehow he cannot seem to hear her.

On shaky legs he moves to the truck, hops in and tries to get it to start. The key jitters in his fingers.

"Come on, *please*." The girl is holding her baby firmly against her chest, choking the movements of the tiny fists, the tiny quavering arms. The key turns in his hand, as if he is not doing it at all, and he watches himself swing the truck in a tight circle, sending up a cloud of red dust. The chickens scatter.

"Is everything okay?" He looks over at her. He has managed to get them back out on the highway, after two wrong turns, and the whole time she has said nothing, just let the baby wail in her arms.

"You can let us out wherever you find a pay phone."

He nods a little and looks back at the road. Small gas stations slide by; pick-ups with cardboard signs selling Vidalia onions or The World's Biggest Pecans by the side of the road; liquor stores with flickering neon lights; green signs that say *Birmingham, 47*, splattered with dried mud. The air whips through the cab of the truck and a strand of hair tickles his ear. His heart has slowed now, and he feels hungry. He has almost decided that if the first place with a pay phone is a fast-food restaurant, he will offer to buy her lunch. But she leans forward, points at a humble grocery store with a phone on the wall next to the shopping carts. He nods, barely, and the pebbles of asphalt crunch beneath his tires as he pulls off. The wind gushing through the windows dies quickly.

"Thank you, Holden." The baby whines, blinks in the sunlight streaming through the windshield and falling across their soft bodies. "I'm sorry about all of this."

"Hey, it's no problem. Honest."

He rests his fingers against the steering wheel and watches the big blue eyes. She squirms as the girl opens the door, reaches across to his cup holder and grabs a couple quarters.

"Can I? Thanks."

He nods and watches the baby, clinging to her mother's arms, the soft golden curls sticking out around her face. The door shuts and the girl drops the two coins into the slot of the phone, bouncing the baby in her arms with her back to him. Under the battered hood, the engine of the truck rumbles. He puts his hands on the steering wheel but does not move, just watches the curves of her back, the baby clutching her shoulder, the way both heads of hair glisten in the harsh sun.

"Baby? You gotta come pick me up."

He feels funny listening, but feels funny thinking of driving away, just leaving them here like that. The windows of the store are caked in dust and everything seems so forsaken.

"Some grocery store on 20. I dunno," she says, stretching her head back, trying to find a sign. "We're just on the other side of Sand Pike, I think."

The sliding door of the grocery store beeps and slides open; someone walks out and their cart bumps off the curb into the parking lot. He feels the heat wrapping around him again, the heavy air sticking to the inside of his lungs. The baby finds him again with her eyes, lets out a small gurgle and holds out her chubby arm.

"Maria? No, she's here with me. No, I told you I could handle him, Baby. Yeah, yeah, just come and get us." The girl notices the hum of the engine, turns her head over her shoulder and raises her eyebrows at him. *Thanks*, she mouths, and nods her head to tell him to go.

A fat cloud rolls in front of the sun and drapes a shadow over them. "Maria," he whispers slowly, almost unspoken to himself and finally puts the truck in drive, drifting away with puffs of dust and one last lingering glance at her tiny fist, clenching a handful of her mother's shirt.

Norman Fischer

FROM ON A TRAIN AT NIGHT

Finally things matter—that they do
Flipped-through meanings unstated
Or stated merely in reverse
As the relentlessly organized
Gives way to the flimsy and forced

O soul! How speak frankly
Of this, explain learnedly away
As if a vase of flowers the whole enchilada
Of fate or God or law or fun
And utter desolation

No matter what they do's tragically understated—
And time, reversed, is organized and free

~

Finally all this beauty fades—finally time
Stands, demands its due
And does remain sated
As moments are
Once they've been stripped
Of their named desires   Whole days float out
On this ministry of palms and roses—
You simply can't beat back a beach with its insistent
Torque producing confidence and indignation
Sufficient to snap into presence these scattered configurations
And feel, as you once did, alive to the experience

~

Gray-white days incessant pound
Time's gaps like eyes in weeks'

Heads—how many more till we're dead
Again like roses in a vase red
Buds limply lean on lip
Petal-serrated, and seeing's
Glow so sure just then and now
Arriving pure as silk or thyme
Again raises its palm for world's shout—
Living's carefully casual orchestration
Of colors now fade in and out the eye
Of wind, of crinkled leaf, of driven snow—
No—hear this in that:
A fallen need
To pull the plug
Of going on being
Again

~

Gash in everything all the time
Breathing in the source for instance
The simple fact of my not being no matter what
Another but still as ever the one I am
Swimming the permanent dream of being myself
As neck at the end of rope or sands
At the end of time tethering me to my
Interventions

Hard to say how I sink in the heft of it
This dance that couldn't be that or the next
I wear a shirt enough to recall (that I
Know to put it on at all) the ardor of having been
And going on being long enough or not
If such a phrase has any sense now that
These lines are erased at last by the hands
Whose fingers' pen
Scratches against a range of silences

However one makes that this deploys
Depends on forward-rolling listening

Not controlled from alone or inside but tethered
Outward as a rope joins knotted a range of objects
It hold in tow till all disgorge in hence

~

How about that—nothing in particular
Sways out there in the wind all the tendrils move
In each which ways
As if inclement weather daunts them
To a halting stalling just as the beam
Of my wanting what could not be desire's
Object blunts me pulling me along
On its blathering furor—
            It's hard not to walk against the grain
In this creepy world
We cradle in our weary arms
With its lush water rushing at you
Hard to entertain being washed out with it
Again as one way but apparently
Forgot, what with the distracting meals and
Airy sorrows of the day—herewith a grasping
Of syllables or any air at all—that would be
The worst: without any air at all

~

Hole into an original world
You climb up from and can't return
Smoke wafting into air from fire below
Word-stones hurled from cliffs above
Split into pieces—earth teeters
Off course—bulked clouds with fuzzy fingers
Shooting out of them—gray smudges of arrested rain

Sky's spread out
Like puzzle pieces on a table
Something about to occur
But doesn't—this never-occurring

Potential is what is—
Halt between in and out, is and not,
Bowed, blown, music, categories shattered

~

It wants peace and quiet
Sometimes to learn one thing
So as to forget it

Nearly dimmer, then later
A stupor sets in
Whenever I toll this bell

That lingers and is limber
I can touch the runners
As they course by carrying me

Too hot to touch
But you can't not wonder
For you need the food

How they make their rounds
On their lilting numbers
Is abstract on their hearths

I do not know and cannot concur
Only reconcile their books and plunder
Call out on high for help

~

In those eyes the words spill over
Before the thought there's water
Unstable and flowing that eats the edges
Quiet out beyond the breakers
In the definite crescent or in the craters
There's casting up of weight in the swell
So that looking into them there is no contact
Outside the sheer warmth that that is there

Present in the larger vicinity
The collision is immanent
A force pressing over you unannounced
Of memory back to the beginning
Which is carried along with the effortless floating
Sky and sea make an edge of it
That you reach out toward with your hand
But only sense in the sound of the words
Sound of waves like tinkling glass on beaches
Like those eyes of light so deep back going
There's no connecting, no escape

~

In the haze
When before there was full moon
Hung out over water
I'm talking again tapped
By the muttering birds
That have engendered small details
How I live related to the picture
Above of me returning
How to mend the mind's beauty
All that wonders or sings
How generous the table and cup are
The book, the bell, the sandal
Your auburn eyes the struggle
And sorrow of your burnt beginnings

~

I wandered into the place unawares
And was immediately given a number and a scorecard—
Now—how to distance myself from the crowd

Was it a matter of diet or hygiene?
Was it wardrobe, coiffure, interior decoration?
Was it a question of what I believed or thought I knew?
Was it who (however you'd set that one up, block on block) I actually was
Or appeared to be?

At night I slipped away to watch baseball under the stars
My ancient boyhood myth chthonic blood throb
Or was that scars, the abrasive unfolding of the past against my very skin
Now only engraved upon the air in fleeting lunging images?

No matter how hard I tried I could never think of it
Without thinking of something propelled by the force
Of my confusion, justice, a penchant for improvement and perfection—
The heart melts down when that substance is exuded
When the things I've been writing about all through time
(Without thinking about it all my memories erased)
Proved to be so passé already over-exposed and over-determined
And I'd had to learn a new language just to recover my socks
Which I had left outdoors on the railing of the last city on the tour

Many times I have wondered what was really in that trunk
I'd kept ready all those years, forgotten mementos I planned to take back with me
On my eventual return when all of the past as I had imagined it
Would snap back in a rush of colorful pictures tumbling over themselves
The reds, the blues, the greens, the yellows
This pale pink pathetic poetry I've been saving up for in the middle of this dream
For the flamboyant extravaganza at the end
When I wake up into another less rudimentary world—

Well that turned out to have been not the case at all—
I was still, afterward, here, even after all that fuss and sorrow
And to say I always was or will be or constantly am is something I will certainly necessarily
Do   and the words will make it true
And even believable
In their military arrangements
And you too—stitched together with dental floss because that was all we had
Without any idea of where we really were
Or any actual idea at all

~

I'm sitting again in the hospital
It is day
There's a flower on the table a purple orchid
Amid ferns

Under skylight
A piano with no piano
Player plays into smooth air
As people speak a hushed counter-melody

Meanwhile
Strapped into bed in a terrible storm
You negotiate a lifetime of torn leaves
In your body's twitching dream-drone contusions

Time's a thread a light beam in a window
Voices, disappointments, disintegrations
Blind rage diffused in silence
A healing grace

(for Paul Yockey)

~

Nathan Hauke

AFTER MUSIC THE MUSIC OF CHIMES AND KEROSENE

3/16
John 3:16

Reckoning
A shed's fract/
ured truss
Pinned to
Thrown
Corrugated
Tin sheet

An eye, a
Dirty
White
Buck-
Et
Wedged in a   pocket of roots
Made to catch   whatever
Redeemed by   shadows of budded branches
That drift   over a column on the floor
Another current   muted by a smudged surface
Trash strewn   deck of the trailer

Nathan Hauke

GUNSHOTS UP THE RIDGE

Bloom into handsome black mare
Miscreant neighbor kids hack at the field's weedy border
With archaic golf clubs. Nobody to raise them
Who was it told you wasps drill right into the body of the cicada
Count yourself one among so many blessings
A vessel to be filled and laid to waste
Wall of a burned-out condo crumbling around what's left of the chimney

Nathan Hauke

TINDER IS A HATCHET JOB

P/ *p*R / *r*I/ *i*S/ *s*M/ *m*S/ *s*
While light cuts into the layered stalks of weeds
A catechism poor as purple thistle
Wide distance from ash to black fur
Measured in countless thin yellow flowers
Silence a dusty hymnal
~~For love of music—~~
Grown rich to the ears
As wind in a cross-pattern fence

Pink shred of ribbon tied to a branch near a corroded bottle cap
Where I piss into the brush

Nathan Hauke

PHYSICS

All I'm saying is

It takes a certain amount of electricity

To regrow a bone

Broke a window in the flowerbed
And oozed in through a crawlspace under the house
Nosing a leathery snail with a fractured shell under wet leaves
Blamed the dealers who lived across the dirt road from the trailer
No one was worried about the stuff that was stolen
They were worried about the guns (heirlooms)
Shattered glass amber in memory
Catches light like an old toy in a wooden box

You leave it for the next one comes along

Jesse Sensibar

ONE MORE REASON NOT TO SLEEP WITH PEOPLE YOU DON'T KNOW VERY WELL

I'm sorry I couldn't stop to chat right there in the frozen pizza and ice cream aisle. But my head was in a different space—not so well-lit. I would have had to tell you about the crosshairs of Allah dancing on my shoulder blades like a ditch I couldn't reach.

You wanted to tell me about Buddha and reincarnation—I saw it in your brown eyes. But all I could hear coming from your pretty, pink-lipsticked mouth was Sitting Bull saying, "Today is a good day to die."

So I just bought my frozen juice bars and went back to my pony.

Because it is a good day to die but tomorrow might be a little brighter.

If I had told you all this, would you still say I had an old soul?

Jesse Sensibar

A DEMON STALKS THE LAND, LITANY OF PRAISE

He and Sonny would laugh every time they'd lose another one. "Yeah, he couldn't keep up" was what they'd say. Because he was just a big old turkey buzzard circling over this town, floating on thermals of sadness, addiction, meth and ruin.

For twenty years the bodies fell all around him and he picked at the broken bones of dis-repair and despair. He'd laugh and grin and snarl, "It's hard to starve a buzzard out 'cause he ain't particular about what he eats."

He'd get head from Rose at *The Twilight* while her children watched –then glass pipe nod and sleep for twenty hours straight.

Behind every outwardly functional and successful addict a predator is crouched who won't hesitate to eat its own young.

Sometimes he cooked in the kitchen, sometimes the back porch. Red phosphorous stains still bleed through paint

He worked both sides of the line, cut it right down the middle. Made sure nobody trusted him and everyone was afraid. It broke his heart and blackened an oily soul scorched rusted dreams while he laughed, too high to care.

He took what he could and crushed what he couldn't and laughed when they called him insane. He walked through the valley of the shadow of death and emerged damaged but unharmed.

There is an old man with D batteries duct taped to his head microwaving half gallons of ice cream at the Shell station.

Jesse Sensibar

SAVED

Monica Rojas. You met her and dated her briefly just out of high school when she was scooping ice cream at The Sweet Life and body building professionally. Later, when she became a stripper at Shaky Drakes where you worked the door keeping an eye on the customers and making sure all the girls were safe, you saw her become the most fantastic exotic dancer you had ever seen and you realized she was way too big for this little town. Didn't realize it then but she was way too big for this little planet as well. You stayed in touch and always loved her from afar. She hit the road but would send you copies of all the dirty magazines she appeared in. She would call you sometimes in the middle of the night when you woke up wrestling with your own demons and tell you that she just knew from hundreds or thousands of miles away that you needed to talk. It was funny how she always knew, funny how many nights she saved you.

So the pain was that much more intense when you found out she had died with nothing and nobody but a fifth of vodka and a bottle of pills to keep her warm in her expensive apartment in Dallas and the anger at the possibility that maybe she didn't die alone still smolders deep.

Juan Parra

WE

I was outside the Karl Marx theatre drinking Rum and Coke when a hyena walked up to me and urinated on me. It was mostly brown with gray spots on the legs. I started to pet it and it licked my fingers. I was fascinated but felt a bit fearful and even wondered if I was going nuts. I started thinking about getting a leash and a collar. People looked stunned. "It's not mine," I pleaded. "It came to me." "A hyena in a Cuba!" People were stunned- It sat next to me and started licking my face. I felt that she was cleaning the spots of seriousness that sometimes molded my face into a mask of shadows whose heaven drowns in a second. A pest control officer Came over to me and asked if all the vaccines were updated. "It came to me," I said. The officer leaned forward to pet it and it bit off his finger, crushing his wrist in the process. He looked at me and started to cry. "My heart is broken," he said. "It was you that risked it," He sobbed and then stood up and said: "What are you going to name it?" "Sweetheart," I said. "Jesus fucking Christ, This fucking country turn more and more bubble gum by the minute. Everywhere you turn there are people shouting 'I love you' from Balconies, or crying while plucking a rose, or calling savage animals Sweetheart, or, or saying stuff like 'oops I did it again.' And then you have me, who Always wanted to have a pet but makes a living killing them. Please forgive me if I start crying again." "That's fine," I said. "And let me tell you that soon a sweetheart will come your way." We walked towards the dark infested streets, where the lights are forced off early in the evening, and the stench of sweat snakes up the nose and pokes the nostrils, and we walked towards this reality, delightfully dressing and rolling our minds on the syrup of our creamy, caramelized hearts.

Juan Parra

POEM ABOUT LIARS

The groom braids his mother's pleas in thin knots,
As if they were meant for a mannequin
Whose head had fallen off
With the weight of thick hair.

The bride baptizes her lover's image
In the dense darkness of her pupils,
Walks the church packed with inebriated Christians
With strawberry smudges on her teeth.

The crowd smells of sweat and booze
And, they smell each other's ears,
Flick sweat at one another and wear blindfolds,
Until the priest offers his dentures as a sacrament for all to lick.

The lens is broken argues the photographer.

No more pictures of curvy blondes wearing pink dresses.
No more crying mothers with raw onions on their plates.

We have only the promise of eternity to lie about.

Juan Parra

WAITING FOR SUPERMAN

1

The raft was jammed
My sister hugged her bible.
I begged my mother for a Superman Action figure
As soon as we arrive in America.
Make sure to vomit outside, she would whisper to me.
That summer tasted of salt water and vomit,
And the heat made our pores throb
While my father worried for our tired, sad limbs.

2

A tempest formed in the distance,
The wind rapped hard on our faces,
The gray grinded our hopes in a butcher's grinder.

3

Pray to whoever will save us and repent later, cried my sister.
We were nothing but human crumbs on a colossus dappled with spew.
Jabbing breaths raked my lungs; saliva crawled up from my exhausted glands
Flooding my mouth with puke, forcing my cheeks to bloat before release
Leading to another cycle of hard breaths like Christ on the cross,
Nails crushing his hands, his feet, his blessed emaciated feet.

4

My mother held on to me as if I was going to turn into a memory,
A tear claiming a heaven won by age,
A past, a future not realized, a child stripped from her arms by malicious waves,
A pile of clothes drenched in urine and puke,
A collection of shredded limbs, a boy with a wrinkled face and thinning hair
No longer asking for Superman, but for an assurance of life, she could not grant.

Julie Hensley

EVEN STONES COME TO REST:

—Julia Pastrana Considers Her Final Homecoming

I. Mother Tongue

In the camp of my girlhood
burros stomped and brayed
beneath a bower of ocotillo,

and dogs, half feral, tracked
the dust of expired fires.
Quite common: a child's bones

cracked by breech birth;
small limbs, shrunken further
with the scorpion's sting;
madness unleashed
from a poisoned tinaja.

Who would question this dark,
bearded child, *hija fea?* No one,
not once they watched me bend
firm over the yucca root
or walk long in the desert sun.

But who would hold tight to this hand
when offered such wealth?

II. Moonflower

The creamiest bloom
only at nightfall, so he came
to me in darkness. With the rough skin
split, every pitahaya reveals glistening fruit.

Gold throws humiliation into shadow,
and even my corsets were embroidered
with its shimmering threads.

An education:

in the unlacing. I sought
to absorb all I could,
knowing much
can rise up from the shaded,
lluvial plain—aware that

come monsoon season,
every cut bank washes away.

III. Moskva

I thought the child might
anchor me. For a moment,
snow feathering the glass
blurred beneath a narrow finger
of sunlight, transforming my cell
into a sparkling map of the entire world.

But when a late cold spell
froze carriage wheels to stone
and my gowns could no longer be
altered, our days begin to steep—
wood smoke and cabbage soup.

The chamber maid told me
that Russia feasts early,
and I dared imagine a bare crucifix
above my bed, labor's heat
pushing the arched branches of
Chestnuts into pale green bud.

How could I have known
that, cracked by fever,

we would both splinter
into pieces too small, too sharp,
to ever properly retrieve?

IV. Lirio

The prickly globe of cholla
is carried many miles
on the bristled haunch of the javelina,
and the bones of mice may desiccate
years before the spotted owl
pushes the pellet into hot sunlight,

but everything returns home.
Even stones
come to rest in the belly
of the canyon.

Dusted by lilies, my coffin shimmers
and waits. *Mijo*, for a lock
of your dark hair, I would sacrifice
even this attempt at dignity.

The voice of the wind, pollen-scented,
will lull us all to sleep eventually—
    this earth never stops
        grinding itself into sand.

Julie Hensley

LITTLE DEATHS

—Jackie Kennedy Explains her Composure to the American Public

You want to milk my suffering
as if I were a viper, enough antidote
to nurse this entire country
warm inside my painted mouth.

When the berm holds, you fish
suspicion out of the stop-bath—
my suit like peppermint, my wig suddenly
obvious, blood spots on my hem.

What you don't suspect: I wanted
only to hold his head in place
for the moment it took
to say goodbye just as I was

permitted to hold our first daughter—
palm her gray cheek, run my finger
tip along the points of her quiet
spine, barely formed.

Patrick, the one who would
meld us into recognition again.
Though he survived two days,
would you believe I never held him
living, only heard his cry?

And the others—didn't you
know?—I held them in my own way.
A subject no lady should raise,
not even at home, but I have many times
touched that same rusted loss
in the crux of my panties.

So well a wife already knows the stillness
of her husband's breath and pulse.
Often, I watched the jagged flutter
of that pale triangle of flesh
hidden to you by his collar, and
always I saw the same skin settle.
I have resurrected this love before,
Dei Gratia. But a delicate seam
can be stitched only a few times.

You want to crack it like a book cover
shoddily printed, but a mother
knows how to read grief then turn it aside,
so that it might feather, become
merely a page in a much longer story.

Julie Hensley

BLACKWORK SOLSTICE

—Mary Tudor, July 1555

The women gathered here have begun to whisper.
Dark silk through pale linen: they pull the thread
with such fervor. Suspicion rattles the damp air
without cease, just as rain pelts the stained glass.

Dark silk through pale linen: they spread kohl
across powdered skin that I might face another day.
Without cease, just as rain pelts the stained glass,
I plea to Saint Margaret: draw forth the pain

across tightened skin that I might face another day.
When trapped beneath labor's heaves, I will still
plea to Saint Margaret: draw forth the pain.
My heart flutters in my chest like blackbirds

rain-trapped beneath the eaves. I will still
when this smock and kirtle phantom-float and a babe's
heart flutters against my chest. Like blackbirds
gathering, Philip's dark beard will descend

when this smock and kirtle phantom-float. A babe
to wrap and rock, tenderness to stave famine's
gathering. Philip's dark bared, your will descend
in the conjoined cries of mother and child.

Rap and rock tender sheaves to stave famine.
Sunlit villagers will thatch the rotted roofs.
In the conjoined cries of mother and child,
a holy kingdom calmed with an heir's promise.

Past sunlit villages' newly thatched roofs,
the men will return from muddy encampments—

a holy kingdom come with the air's promise,
if only something lies beneath this farthingale.

Yea, the men return from muddy encampments,
and the women gathered have begun to whisper—
they perceive only lies beneath this farthingale.
With such fervor, suspicion rattles the damp air.

Julie Hensley

THE WORK OF WOMEN

—Sarah wakes to an empty house

Like breathing sand—
the boy's absence
swirls sleep-stale air
until I cannot fill my lungs.
I rise to shake
his empty bedding
            and hear
the clatter of animals
carved from juniper,
the companions an only child
curls into his blankets.

The two of them might
have gone to gather wood,
allowing an old woman
to sleep and still
fire unleavened loaves
before the risen sun snuffs
the sound of olive leaves,
the scent of water.

            But something else
draws them up the slope
into the gray light,
where I see
them moving now,
one hand shading my eyes,
the other gripping my keffiyeh.
The sun catches the blade
at my husband's side,
and fear cinches my throat,
tightens my limbs—

as suddenly as flax knots
when I shift the loom.

He whose name we dare not
speak—Abraham claims
He will spin generations
from the rough skein of this sand.
But what can a man know
          of lonely?
Not as much as I
who have witnessed blood
wrung from the constant moon
and then the woman
who pounded those stains from the linen
drawn into my husband's arms,
a horizon that failed
to settle into home.

I will utter those syllables now,
not to beseech His intervention,
but to challenge His claim
on what can only really be mine:
He may have rooted
life into a tarnished womb,
but it was I who pushed
the boy into this world,
          teeth clinched
against a sprig of pennyroyal
as my body split like grapes
overripe on the vine.

Hallal,
Abraham will say,
when he returns, eyes shining—
the sunlit splash
from the waterskin
clearing the wall of the well.
I won't remind him
that even bulls pulled by brass rings
are released to drink from the spring

before entering temple gates—
beasts never catch
the scent of fig and pine
until the knife is drawn
and the stones are slick.

In the coming days,
I will devise my own rituals
into a new covenant:
moving the lamp
and my husband's sandals
once his breath settles into sleep,
doubling the dalet knot
for the guarantee
of his sputter and curse
should he rise early.

            But first my boy,
his dark, trembling lashes,
his face pale and smooth as millet
which the two of us, mother and son,
will grind throughout the morning
because I will insist today
that he help me prepare bread—
            the work of women.
That he might lean into my shoulder
as we kneel before the mortar,
That I might, for a moment,
when we rise,
take each of his hands
in mine, if only
to brush the flour from his palms.

Julie Hensley

THESE TERRIBLE TIMES

—The Angel of the House Resurrected, 1941

How I would love to believe
that sound is the scratching of my pen
drawing ink from the well, carving this page into something true.

Or even robins returning to nest beneath the eaves,
but two weeks into March, the twigs gathered last spring molder
like old thatch. Song birds are fewer this year,
though I watch for a flash of red along the garden hedge.

Instead, it is Her footfall which marks the hours,
incessant as the great clock. All winter
She strained to flush me out of the brush.
I hoped the rain would drown her, leave only wet
pieces strewn like leaves along the river path.

But I hear Her this very moment…
sniffing around the hyacinth bed.

Once I was sheltered here,
though She could rise from any damp corner in Monk House.
Back then, She merely shook tarnished silver in the drawers,
lifted linen panels into taunting sails
so that every sunbeam cradled winking dust motes.
She would alight, for a moment, beneath the largest oak
to make evening settle like amber around my nephew's shoulders.

But now She has begun to claw at the walls of this lodge,
loosening the shingle, until even my ideas start to unhinge—I fear I will
lose them all, like fevered teeth, like pearls
snapped from a thread and rolling the parlor floor.

Years ago, I joked that I had killed Her,
but war can resurrect as well as destroy—
even those bren gun trenches along Mount Caburn
offer green shards of bronze, pieces of an Iron Age pendant
which will be strung like a prayer flag in the vault of the British Museum.

I should be safe at last
from the heat which simmered all those years,
dancing Redowa with the moon. I thought I could
burn the desire out of my womb, tear it like an errant page,
but it creeps back: that vine the gardener calls Bittersweet—
ever loosening the knit of the dry stone wall.

What is writing but an act of parturition?

I feed each life. I swaddle and comfort.
When imagination stirs, it is I
who have cast light on the spider's silver web.
I suffer, and I lift my own feet to plunge
over the edge. I follow beyond what shatters,
          all the way into the ground.

Yet critics insist on tracing fragile lines back to expired lovers—
they sketch Clarissa on rice paper and hold her up to Madge.

These days, the air is full of smoke and supplication—
the very things on which She feasts. It might have been
She who blasted the roof from the Mecklenburgh flat.
At the very least, She wields dust and rubble as a private snare.

    Listen to that iron key rattling the latch...
        it flutters like an injured sparrow.

And then suddenly She dares feign absence
when I know She is underfoot, curled like a feather
in the shadows of my skirt. She sighs and passes through me,
wraith-like, yet the narrow bridge groans beneath our weight.

More and more, I wish for the smooth stones
Thoby and I gathered from the strand below Tallund House.

I remember how we placed them along the stoop,
stacked them in our own mysterious language.
We tasted the salt which graced their surfaces
just the same as it did our skin,
the world's edges reduced to briny memory—
so much which water can remove. I would like
to feel that perfect weight again, an anchor
in these terrible times, something I could keep
like a talisman, deep in the pocket of my coat.

Sandy Coomer

THE BLACK ANT

We see it almost at the same time—
a tiny black carpenter ant
on our dead uncle's white suit.

Your eyes widen with a strange mix
of horror and amusement, as if you
can't decide whether to laugh or cry.

It's always hard at times like these,
when emotion hovers between extremes.
That's why the family put out all those pictures

on either side of the casket, ludicrous poses,
funny faces, sideways hats and tongues
sticking out. They want us to laugh,

but to have enough sense to cry
at the right time. It's no wonder,
with these confusing points of etiquette,

that we stare at the ant, as it makes its way
up the lapel and around the collar, both
of us willing the other to do something

before it disappears around our uncle's neck.
Perhaps because you're the oldest
and are used to such responsibility,

you lean into the slick black marble casket,
holding your breath, wrinkling your nose,
mumbling a rigid curse

at the funeral director's lack of decorum,
pinch the ant between forefinger and thumb,
crumble it, crumb-like, to the floor.

We tell each other it came from one of the plants,
but we know the ant was doing what ants do—
dragging death away straight through

the living, even as death poses
huge and incalculable.
We try not to feel so small.

Susanne Davis

DESTINY'S CLOTHES

The day the boy rode into Asheville, a tropical storm was whipping up the coast from Louisiana. Radio announcers in Connecticut cautioned people to stay off the roads even before one drop of rain fell, but Earl Ray and his wife Marilyn were not about to close their country western bar—River Star Ranch—just because of a storm, especially not on the day of the Annual River Star Competition.

They were at the bar that morning when the boy opened the door and the wind whipped in behind him. Marilyn looked past him out into the parking lot, where his old Chevy pickup sat, rounded fenders, rusty runners, dents and all. His truck, his worn blue jeans and scuffed cowboy boots, even the way he filled the doorframe was curious.

He glanced at her and then shook his head. "I want to sing tonight."

Just then, the sky started to rumble and rain pelted the ground, sending dust into the air. Marilyn pulled the boy in and shut the door behind him. His hand was warm and dry, like an electric blanket, where you could feel the electricity running. His eyes lit on Earl coming toward them.

"I guess this storm's going to be a humdinger," Earl said to Marilyn. "They say it's veering inland, coming our way."

The boy focused on Earl, and Marilyn saw his china doll beauty, the blonde hair, clear skin and periwinkle blue eyes narrow to an animal intensity; his features pushed up slightly and his eyes half-closed as he shifted his guitar.

Earl looked at Marilyn.

"He wants to sing," she said.

"Is that so?" Earl looked hard at the boy.

"Yes, sir."

Thunder shook the air. Both Earl and Marilyn jumped, but the boy didn't flinch.

Earl tipped his head to the side, as if changing perspective would help him figure the boy out. "I'm sorry. We get only name bands, top performers for the competition. People pay $16 a ticket or more to get in here."

"That's what I'm going to be." The boy turned to the almost empty room. "One of the best. I can fill this house now, I bet."

"What's your name?"

"Willie Fillmore."

"Willie Fillmore. All due respect, son, but I never heard of you and I know most people in the business if they're that good. You're telling me you can fill this house?"

The boy nodded.

Earl plunked the armful of linens he was holding onto the table. "Alright then, let's have one song. Make it your best." He eased himself into a chair. Marilyn sat next to him.

"Doesn't matter what I play," the boy said as he opened his guitar case. "They all sound good." He pulled out a shiny red and white guitar.

Marilyn smiled. "You are full of piss and vinegar! You remind me of my husband," she nudged Earl's leg, but Earl was watching the boy. "You go ahead and sing for me and I'll give you a plate of ribs, on the house."

Willie tossed his head; fit the strap over his should and plucked a few strings of the guitar. He opened his mouth and started to sing.

Earl's arm slipped off the back and Marilyn's chair as the boy's mouth emitted sound—a blast of wind forced through a winding tunnel of rock. And the wind, his voice, was like antiquity. It riveted Earl to his seat. He didn't know the song; he wasn't paying attention to the words. He listened to the voice. The boy's voice came rushing on the air high and low pitched, free and focused at the same time.

Earl's face turned fish belly white and sweat broke out above his lip. That boy had a voice as pure as only one other voice he'd ever heard. It was old as rock and young as new breath, and borne up by a spirit not of this world. The boy knew he held power over both of them, but it was Earl he watched, while at the same time compelled by something outside their vision and knowledge. When he finished singing he took a slight bow.

"Boy," Earl cleared his throat and the word came out as a growl, "where'd you get a singing voice like that?"

"It's in the family," Willie said.

Earl sat back, mouth open and shook his head.

Marilyn touched his shoulder. "Earl? Earl? Are you alright?"

Earl didn't speak. He couldn't speak. He wasn't there. He was in the hot New Orleans sun, in a fallow field of cotton, the magnificent pecan trees waving in the wind; Spanish moss draped from each like a lacy shawl on a ghost. Earl gulped down some air. "Yes," he croaked.

Marilyn shifted her attention from Earl back to Willie. "Your family must be so proud of you."

"My mother died a few months ago. Pancreatic cancer." Now his eyes were moist with tears; but behind the tears, they were clear.

Earl winced.

"Oh, that's an awful thing for a boy your age," Marilyn crooned. She wasn't looking at Earl, she was thinking of her own children surrendered to her first husband, surrendered because she had messed up, not through abuse but neglect. The kids were old enough now for the scars to show. But it seemed they didn't think they had scars as long as she stayed out of their lives. She didn't even know what they looked like. "How old are you, Willie?"

"Eighteen," he answered. That was the age of her own son.

"Your daddy?" Earl leaned toward the boy. "What about him?"

"Never knew him," Willie stopped abruptly.

Marilyn put her hand on Earl's arm. "Earl, can we put him on the roster?"

Earl squirmed on his chair like he was sitting on 100 volts. He rubbed his hands on his thighs. "Alright, then. Come back at six o'clock."

Willie nodded and put away his guitar. He turned to leave.

"Willie," Earl called him back. "How did you know about River Star Ranch?"

The boy's eyes narrowed. "Like you said, sir, you're a name in the industry."

Earl puffed up. "I used to be. In New Orleans. Then I met Marilyn and I had to save her from her evil ways. He smirked but hurt washed over Marilyn's face.

She kept her voice light and replied "Earl, I have been saved by a higher power than capital Y-O-U."

Earl smiled at her, a tight little smile. "I don't think so, Marilyn."

"I know so." Marilyn shook her head to wipe away the pain, then smiled bravely at the boy. "Earl had a place on Bourbon Street," she said, with pride.

"You heard of Bourbon Street?" Earl shot at Willie.

"Sir, I was born on Bourbon Street." Willie turned away again.

Marilyn followed him to the door. Looking back, she saw Earl staring after the boy. The lunch crowd had begun to appear, needing her attention, but she ran into the kitchen and dialed her friend Carmel, a psychic down in New Orleans.

"Carmel, honey. Do you have a minute? The strangest thing just happened—a boy just came in…" She told Carmel about Willie and his voice and its effect on Earl.

When Marilyn was finished talking, Carmel said, "Listen Marilyn, it's time we talked portals. We never talked about this before, but there are points of energy in your body, places located on the back of your body, which get ignored. Portals, they're called. Always been there, and almost always been ignored. People who pray or meditate can turn their awareness around, open up these areas so to speak and open to other realities through the portals. Sometimes visitors even come through the portals to help people with their unfinished business. Don't be afraid. You still pray regular, don't you?"

"Yes, I do," Marilyn said proudly. "Every day I get a good conversation going with Jesus."

"Well, I'm getting a strong signal from you up there. Now, listen good. It shouldn't be too hard for you to do this. What you need to do is open up the portal this boy came through to find out why he's here. Can you do that?"

"What is this portal? I don't understand."

"You may not understand it until you do it, sugar. But I think this boy has some business with you and Earl."

"Well, Carmel," Marilyn looked over the kitchen staff from the corner where she was hunched, and lowered her voice. "There is something strange here, that's for sure. You just never heard anything like this boy's voice. I never have. It doesn't sound human. You should see Earl. He seems hypnotized. I never saw him look the way he's looking now. It took some hold of him.

"This boy must have sensed some splinter need you two have," Carmel said. "It's probably not a core need, not yet, which is good, because then you'd really have problems. But still, splinter needs radiate from the core so you got to recognize them."

Just then there was a crack of thunder interrupted.

"Me and Earl are fine," Marilyn said.

"Maybe. Maybe not." Carmel's voice crackled through the line, and then she hung up without even saying goodbye. Marilyn was used to that. Carmel was her only friend left from New Orleans and they talked about once a month. Whenever Marilyn told Carmel she missed her, Carmel, instead of agreeing, would say, "I'm right here with you, honey," as if time and distance weren't real.

Marilyn looked out at the dining room again. Earl was still there, sitting in his trance.

"Hey Marilyn?!" the cook shouted. "Maybe you'd like to take out these plates?"

Marilyn grabbed the entrées and took them out, leaning over to kiss Earl on the head as she passed by. He moved out from under the caress of her lips. She found him a few minutes later in the supply room, stacking linens.

"Earl, what are you doing in here? You've got to get to the bank and get the prize check before noon." It was like he was sleepwalking.

They had been married for 18 years, 16 of them in Asheville. When they moved up north and opened River Star Ranch, Earl thought he had left his ghosts behind. But that boy was a ghost, he was sure of it.

"I'm going to get the check in plenty of time, Marilyn," he snapped now. "Just leave me alone." It had taken him years to reconcile himself to this place, to the smallness of it compared to Bourbon Street. The boy's appearance reawakened his disappointed sense of destiny.

Marilyn stood under the light and Earl noticed with distaste the gray roots of her hair and the sagging skin under her chin. She took a deep breath. "I don't know why you say things to hurt me, Earl, but I'm not going to try to hurt you back. I know you've got disappointments. We all get disappointed in life, but that doesn't mean you just pass it on, especially to the person who loves you."

That was classic Marilyn. She laid her vulnerability at his feet for him to step on or respect. He saw she had prepared his stage outfit as she called it silver-studded belt, his cowboy hat, and a checked shirt pressed and neatly folded on a shelf next to the old red cowboy boot from which he would draw the winner's name.

When Earl looked back to the door, the space Marilyn had occupied was empty.

"I know your mother's name," he whispered to the wind. "Her name is Alyson Brand."

✦

Earl's bar had been on Bourbon Street. He waited for the time of day when the music started, when he could stand on the uneven sidewalk and hear the air fill with its music. The saxophones, trumpets, drums like spirits floating filling the sky, swirling over head, swooping down to enter his bar, his ears, his soul. The music was joy, joy, joy.

And that was how he met Alyson Brand. She was with a gig coming through New Orleans for a month. That first night she sang and he heard her voice, the same voice as the boy's now—exactly that voice without gender, not owned by sex, unfettered from the world. His whole life had prepared him for her because he expected love to come like a thunder bolt, not low and grounded and quiet, as it had with Marilyn. He and Marilyn had been married for one unremarkable year. As soon as he saw Alyson, with her platinum hair scooped up and held by a clip in the back, except for a few wispy strands that hung down and caressed her neck and then heard her sing, he fell in love. That first night after her gig they closed his bar and still found places to go.

"I should go back to the hotel and rest my voice," she said. It was nearly eight in the morning. Instead they walked to Café Du Monde, where a swarm of people gathered under the canopy in Jackson Square, voices animated and happy. The waiter brought them chicory coffee and a plate of hot beignets with powdered sugar heaped on top and Earl and Alyson watched the birds swoosh down to the empty tables and peck at the sugary crumbs. By 9 am the jazz started and voices rose and fell with the beat. He liked the way Alyson tossed her head, like she was shaking the music around all the time. A saxophone player had played "Smile and the world smiles with you," and Alyson had sung along. All talking stopped. All eyes were on her. Earl felt proud to be with her.

The month had gone by in a blur. She was 28 to his 43. Every night, he listened to her sing and every day, he shared all the people in his life with her, including all the music connections. Earl hardly went home and it wasn't long before Marilyn knew of the affair but Earl didn't care. He had never felt so alive, so connected to a purpose a reason for doing everything he did, every minute of the day…and night. He took Alyson to the best bars, the places where people played.

One night after hot music and hotter sex, they lay in her hotel room watching the sun come up and Earl said "This weekend I'm going to tell Marilyn I'm leaving her."

"What?" Alyson shook her head, her objection clear. "Why?"

"Because of us? For us. " He reached for her hand.

She pushed him away. We never talked about this. I'm going to Nashville, Earl. This is…well, this is just what it is."

He saw then that she thought she was poised on the edge of greatness, stretching into her future success and leaving him far in the background.

"But you'll need a home to come back to, wherever you go." He hated how weak he sounded but he said it anyway. He couldn't lose her.

She flung his arm off her and sprang off the bed. The next day she left New Orleans and every day, he waited for her to return. Months on end. Marilyn hovered over him, but he wouldn't speak about it. How could Alyson disappear after she had made him love her like that, plan his whole life around her? She was like fog lifting off the road during a rainstorm. She was night itself. But still, he waited for her to come back. His business faltered. Alyson cut a record and it sold but not well. He thought she might come back then. No. More months stretched on. Then Marilyn's uncle died and she inherited the house in Asheville. She told him she was leaving and he needed to make a choice. He didn't see it as much of a choice. He felt dead either way.

What if—. Now Earl knew this might sound crazy, but not so crazy. What if this boy was his son? He and Marilyn had not had any children together. What if Alyson had gone off and had this baby and never wanted to tell him—who knew why. But it would be like her. Why else would this boy be here now? He wanted to believe—this boy was family.

Marilyn waited for him to leave for the bank, and then she slipped away from the lunch crowd, into the back room and locked the door. She sank down onto the floor, and slowed her breath, trying as Carmel had told her to send all that energy flowing around to the back of her body, instead of stopped up in her head. The storm had kicked up again, the wind whining and crying like a baby. Just like a baby, stuck alone in some room, whining and crying. Marilyn started to cry, remembering how her children had clung to her when Family Services came to take them away. They were so young. She was just 22 and the kids were 2 and 3. She had stopped dancing at the Sky Top when she had the kids but she was hooked on the drugs and she did what she needed to get them. Her first husband had given her chances, she couldn't say he hadn't. And she had blown every one. Earl came along and helped her back on her feet. Forgiving him had become practice for forgiving herself, but there were days, like this one, when she wondered why she bothered.

At 5:30, the sky was pitch black. The storm thrashed and moaned, but still River Star Ranch was filling up with out of towners. Many of the singers were going to be late, the storm had delayed flights and downed power lines had prevented others from getting there and Earl was in a foul mood.

When Willie appeared wearing the same outfit as earlier with the addition of a black cowboy hat pulled low over his eyes, Earl and Marilyn approached from opposite sides of the restaurant. Earl reached him first.

"A bunch of people on the roster are stuck in traffic. Can you sing?"

Willie looked around the restaurant and his face was a screen, but when he nodded, Earl could see her profile again. The aquiline nose, the straight brows, the chiseled chin.

"Was Alyson Brand your mother?" He blurted it out.

"Who?" Willie frowned.

"Are you serious? Earl" Marilyn asked. "After all these years—?"

The boy's gaze went between the two of him. Earl was still convinced that the boy was his son.

Marilyn stepped back; the plate of hot ribs she was carrying slid to the floor.

"You don't deserve me, Earl. You never did." She spun away and left the ribs splattered on the floor.

"Marilyn, come back here and clean that up," Earl shouted.

Willie jammed his hat on his head.

A tremendous crack of thunder split the air. The lights flickered, and then went out.

"Oh, shit," Earl stomped his foot. In the pitch black he could see nothing. "Stay seated everyone. Give me two minutes to get to the basement and turn on the generator." He lowered his voice and whispered, "Willie? Can you sing for them? Something to keep them occupied so they don't panic?"

"Sure thing, sir," Willie answered.

Earl clapped his hands together. Even in pitch darkness he could feel the people's restlessness. "Stay seated. Please. Mr. Willie Fillimore is going to sing for you while I go start the generator." Earl backed away, arms reaching for the wall behind him. He found the door and eased his way down the stairs and around the all to the generator. Just before he flipped the switch and heard the familiar hum of electricity, just for a moment, he paused to listen to the boy's voice. Without the benefit of sight, his other senses shifted into play and the voice, while beautiful and pure did not sound like the voice he remembered. It sounded tinny now, like an adolescent's undeveloped soprano. Why had he thought otherwise? How had that voice held such power? Was it Destiny itself, come to correct his life choice? His heart pounded and he was having trouble breathing.

He started the generator and light flooded the basement. Pushing open the doors of the bulkhead, he scrambled up the steps and let the rain pelt him. There was no moon, but outside he could breath. By the light of the generator, he followed the stone walk to the front door of the restaurant. He could see Willie singing now. Through the window, he could see that the boy was standing in the center of the room, holding the microphone, turning each time he sang a few phrases. He sang as if the entire room was his stage. The people clapped and Earl saw the joy on the boy's face, a face that no longer looked like Allyson Brand's face. This Willie Fillmore, who lit the room like a celestial body, was a stranger to him.

Marilyn came from the kitchen and stood in the corner of the room. Her white shirt cast her skin in a sallow light, showing the dark circles beneath her eyes. She looked tired; she worked so hard in the bar, not because she loved it, but because she loved him. He watched as she closed her eyes. Her lips moved. Was she praying?

He felt foolish, haunted by the ghost of a memory of a woman who had never loved him, who had used all his musical connections and disappeared from his life, while his wife had taken him back, forgiven him and worked by his side to make his dream a reality for all these years. What a terrible betrayal of her love he had just committed.

He moved toward the door.

Marilyn's eyes fluttered open and she glanced out the window and saw him, soaking wet. She pulled a cloth from the table and met him at the door, wrapping him in it. "You'll catch a death of a cold," she said.

"You are right," Earl said, catching her hand. "I don't deserve you. The truth is, you save me every day Marilyn. I mean it."

"I know," She smiled and patted him with the cloth again. "You think I don't know? Go on in now, Earl. It's you they want, not this pretty boy."

She shoved him into the dining room and all the people turned toward him. Willie was still holding the microphone. Earl plucked it out of his hands.

"I'd like you all to give a hand to Willie." The crowd obliged. "That's some voice on that boy. I'm sure you'll get to be that star you're planning on becoming."

The door opened and their lead act walked in. Earl looked around at the people.

"Just one person I'd like to acknowledge tonight. My wife, Marilyn."

Marilyn stood in the entryway, wiping her hands on her thighs.

"Honey, it's you holding me together. I'm sure all these people know it. I'm sorry it took me so long to see it." He held his arm out for her and she floated toward him and tucked herself in his embrace, the one she had waited so long for.

TJ Beitelman

EVENT HORIZON: OEDIPUS

This is the story of his life he drew up around himself: he fancied himself
a young man who was not a young man at all but one who
was already old or at least a young man who had been aspiring to
advanced years all his life.

> *——a parable: in another world, an Old Man carries the*
> *book of my life in his pocket much as one might carry a*
> *cherished book of poems. There are dog ears. Smudges of grease*
> *where he got his lunch on it. Three pages he rips out and tapes*
> *them to his bedroom wall. Because he loves them so...——*

He thought of himself as a young man who was not a young man at
all but one whose life was already missing three pages.

An old man is a man who rips the middles out of things even or
especially if he loves them.

TJ Beitelman

EVENT HORIZON: METASTASIS

This is the story of his life he drew up around himself: the dog has a hole in her ear or else the hole in her ear is what he imagines will be born when they pluck the black growth from inside it.

Or else she herself will dig it out on accident with her delicate hind-leg scratching.

Which is exactly what happens.

The growth is tender as new growth.

The tender green shoot reaches. A newborn's fingernail is parchment-thin. For a time what bleeds is still alive forever.

TJ Beitelman

THE TALK WITH TALK OF SPORT

This is the story of his life he drew up around himself: Angel said Father I've married the King of the Hardwood and he is so often out of breath and I breathe into him. His long bones ache. All morning is lacing his sneakers. It is more than I believe I can do to make him whole.

There is just so much of him.

He spreads his arms wide.

> *——our arms are not our arms but wings. Our bones not bones but words for bones. Our words are not words but prayers. Five. Four. Three. Two. One.——*

He puts up a prayer and it dances
on the breakaway rim.

TJ Beitelman

EVENT HORIZON: THE MUSE

This is the story of his life he drew up around himself: she stopped midstream.

A sentence is a stream.

A froth of swift-moving ~~sentiment~~—sediment. What unseen creatures thrive there or do not.

He stamped across yon field into a hilly green ~~word~~—wood. To hide.

Hiding is a thing human beings do. All animals do it.

He stepped into the cold stream and up was a whole alley of things leading to the free blue sky.

> *——pretend you know I'm here. Pretend you know I need you to read my mind. Pretend echolocation at least. I came so far and have come so close—close the distance between this and that half of my half-hearted—heart…yes: heart————*

Her mind was a stream. Lord and it was so swift so dark. Beautiful and cold. The body of her words her world. The body of her body.

> *——body is a word for beauty.——*

And so he had no choice but to believe it all was real.

TJ Beitelman

HAIRSHIRT

This is the story of his life he drew up around himself: a collection of personal miscellany and minutiae.

All the bloodless words that had failed him.

Where scars used to be. If it rained on his birthday or a cold Lord's day in June. How much string and spit and gum is useful in a lifetime. Every sales receipt a villanelle a sestina a road map. His time-stamped time. His accounting.

The accounting of his accounting.

There is nothing he can say he fashioned with his hands.

——I gave up trying to
put the world in my mouth one piece at a ime. Only saints should
be so patient or so empty.———

BIOGRAPHIES

TJ BEITELMAN has published a novel, *John the Revelator,* and two poetry collections, *Americana* and *In Order to Form a More Perfect Union,* all of which are available through Black Lawrence Press. His work has appeared in *Indiana Review, Quarterly West, New Orleans Review, Verse Daily,* and *Diagram,* among other publications, and he's been awarded fellowships from the Alabama State Council on the Arts and the Cultural Alliance of Greater Birmingham. He serves as chair of the Creative Writing department at the Alabama School of Fine Arts. He can be found on-line at www.tjbman.com.

AMBROSE BIERCE disappeared in Mexico in 1913. He is known for his short stories and satire (*The Devil's Dictionary*). His excellent story, included here, is considered public domain.

SANDY COOMER is a poet, mixed media artist, and endurance athlete. Her poetry has most recently been published in *Apeiron Review, Red River Review,* and *Pilcrow & Dagger.* Her poetry chapbook, *Continuum,* was published by Finishing Line Press in 2012. Her second collection, *The Presence of Absence,* won the 2014 Janice Keck Literary Award for Poetry. She lives in Brentwood, Tennessee, where she regularly trains for and races triathlons.

SUSANNE DAVIS holds an MFA from the Iowa Writers' Workshop. Her short stories have been published in *American Short Fiction, Notre Dame Review, descant, Zone 3, Carve,* and numerous other journals. Her work has won the Hemingway First Novel Award. She teaches at the University of Connecticut and Trinity College.

DALLAS FLETCHER is a San Francisco Bay Area transplant originally from the Midwest. He has an MFA in creative writing from Mills College in Oakland and writes fiction, poetry, and occasionally grocery lists. His superhero day job is teaching at a special needs preschool for students with emotional and behavioral challenges. He finds inspiration for writing by hiking through the redwoods with his partner Harold.

NORMAN FISCHER is a poet, essayist, and Zen Buddhist priest. A graduate of the University of Iowa Writer's Workshop, his latest poetry collections are *Magnolias All At Once* (Singing Horse, 2015) *Escape This Crazy Life of Tears: Japan 2010* (Tinfish, 2014), *The Strugglers* (Singing Horse, 2013), and *Conflict* (Chax Press, 2012). His latest prose works are the forthcoming (December 2015, from University of Alabama Press), *Experience: on Thinking, Writing, Language and Religion, and Training in Compassion: Zen Teachings on the Practice of Lojong* (Shambhala, 2013).

Brad Garber writes, paints, draws, photographs, hunts for mushrooms and snakes, and runs around naked in the Great Northwest. He has published poetry in *Clementine Poetry Journal, Spank the Carp, Dark Matter Journal, Dirty Chai, Gambling the Aisle, Black Fox Literary Magazine, Ray's Road Review,* and other quality publications. He is a 2013 Pushcart Prize nominee.

NATHAN HAUKE is the author of *Every Living One* (Horse Less Press, 2015), *In the Marble of Your Animal Eyes* (Publication Studio, 2013), and five chapbooks, including most recently *Tinder Is a Hatchet Job* (forthcoming from LRL Textile Series). His poems have been anthologized in *Hick Poetics* (Lost Roads Press, 2015) and *The Arcadia Project: North American Postmodern Pastoral* (Ahsahta Press, 2012).

JULIE HENSLEY'S persona poems, each featuring the voice of a historical or mythical woman who has lost a child in some way, are part of a larger cycle of poems exploring motherhood. Other poems from the cycle have recently been featured in *Saranac Review, Gulf Stream, New Madrid,* and *Southern Women's Review.* A chapbook of her poems, *The Language of Horses,* was published by Finishing Line Press, and a collection of her stories, *Landfall: A Ring of Stories,* is forthcoming from Ohio State University Press. She is a faculty member at Bluegrass Writers Studio, the low-residency MFA Program at Eastern Kentucky University.

HANK LAZER'S nineteen books of poetry include *N24* (2014) and *N18* (2012), *Portions* (2009), and *The New Spirit* (2005). Pages from Lazer's shape-writing handwritten notebooks have been performed with soprano saxophonist Andrew Raffo Dewar in the US and in two concerts in Havana, Cuba. Lazer's Selected Poems in translation will be appearing in books in the coming year in China, Cuba, and Italy. In 2015, Lazer was selected to receive Alabama's most prestigious literary prize, the Harper

Lee Award, for lifetime achievement in literature. For more on the notebooks, see the special online features in *Talisman* #42 and *Plume* #34.

JUAN PARRA is a student finishing a BFA in English from Florida International University. His poems have been published in the *Indiana Review, The Lake,* and *Basalt.*

JESSE SENSIBAR loves small furry animals and assault rifles with equal abandon. In 2014 he earned his MFA in creative writing while teaching freshman composition at a large southwestern state university in the mountain town where he has lived since the late 1980s. His work has appeared in *Ray's Road Review, Fuck Fiction, Corner Club Press, Grey Sparrow Journal,* and *Niche.*

BRIAN L. TUCKER enjoys books by anyone rivaling Marjorie Kinnan Rawlings' *The Yearling,* although few have. His family currently resides in beautiful Chattanooga, Tennessee—home of the Moon Pie and Ruby Falls. Visit him on his Web site: BrianLTucker.com and follow him on Twitter @theBrianTucker.

RACHEL JAMISON WEBSTER directs the Creative Writing Program at Northwestern University. She is the author of the full-length collections of poetry, *September* (Northwestern University Press, 2013) and *The Endless Unbegun* (2015) as well as two chapbooks, *The Blue Grotto* (2009) and *Leaving Phoebe* (forthcoming 2015), both from Dancing Girl Press. Her poems and essays have recently appeared in many journals and anthologies, including *Poetry, Tin House, The Southern Review, The Paris Review, Narrative,* and *Labor Day: Birth Stories from Today's Best Women Writers* (FSG, 2014). You can read more at www.racheljamisonwebster.com.

JESSE LEE WOOTON is the author of *In the Hills, the Garden* (2015) forthcoming from GreencupBooks. He grew up in eastern Kentucky, with an overprotective mother and a disturbing number of cousins. After high school, he spent time at three universities, a community college, a mortician's trade school, and a state hospital for the insane.

www.ingramcontent.com/pod-product-compliance
Lightning Source LLC
Chambersburg PA
CBHW081139300726
48982CB00006B/1007

9781943661039